"*A Confident Heart* showed me how much self-doubt affects every area of my life. This book encouraged me, equipped me, and changed me. Honestly, I think everyone should read it!"—Jill B., Iowa

"Rich with the truth of God's love, compassion, patience, and never-ending supply of power, this book moved me from looking at my past with sorrow to living my future rooted and grounded in the confidence of Christ." —Danielle J., North Carolina

"Through *A Confident Heart* Renee reminded me that I may fail God, but He will never fail me. I love the Scriptures woven into prayers at the end of each chapter. They hold such a wealth of truth! I will continue to use them as daily prayers."—Joy B., Ontario

"*A Confident Heart* gave me courage and clarification to believe in my calling. I now see beauty in my brokenness—something I saw only in everyone else. God used this message to help me to see myself as beautiful in a way I never had before."—Cris N., California

"I practically highlighted whole chapters. Renee helped me see how 'the God of all hope is calling me out of the shadow of my doubts so I can live with a confident heart!'"—Melinda T., Oregon

"*A Confident Heart* moved me from believing what God says about me to receiving it and living in it. One thing Renee taught me is how to 'fail forward' by learning from my mistakes and leaving them behind for good—along with my guilt, shame, and worry!"—Lisa S., Texas

"Renee helped me see that 'salvation is a one-time decision, but finding satisfaction in Christ and living in the security of His promises is a daily process.' I will read *A Confident Heart* over and over to keep it fresh in my heart and mind."—Margaret S., North Carolina

"Renee showed me how 'I can find lasting satisfaction when I continually drink from the source of God's unconditional love.' I'm giving a copy to my daughters and their friends. I wish I'd read this when I was in my twenties. How differently my life may have turned out."—Lelia C., Nebraska

"Reading *A Confident Heart* helped me realize that I'm not alone in my insecurities. I am normal, loved, accepted, and approved by a mighty God."—Tammy N., Kentucky

"I received *A Confident Heart* the week I found out my mom was in her final days on earth. I ended up reading chapters out loud to her. The message was so powerful. The Scriptures were right there. I would say, 'Mom, listen to this!' Renee's words lifted my heart and carried me through."—Kirsten S., Pennsylvania

"In all of my fifty-five years, I've never read a book that spoke to me, moved me, and set me free from so many issues. I couldn't put it down!"—Debbie L., North Carolina

a confident heart

a
confident heart

How to **Stop Doubting Yourself**
and **Live in the Security** of
God's Promises

Renee Swope

Revell

a division of Baker Publishing Group
Grand Rapids, Michigan

© 2011 by Renee Swope

Published by Revell
a division of Baker Publishing Group
PO Box 6287, Grand Rapids, MI 49516-6287
www.revellbooks.com

Repackaged edition published 2021
ISBN 978-0-8007-4031-3

Printed in the United States of America

The Library of Congress has cataloged the original edition as follows:
Swope, Renee, 1967–
    A confident heart : how to stop doubting yourself & live in the security of God's promises / Renee Swope.
        p.   cm.
    Includes bibliographical references.
    ISBN 978-0-8007-1960-9 (pbk.)
    1. Trust in God—Christianity. 2. Confidence—Religious aspects—Christianity. I. Title. II. Title: How to stop doubting yourself & live in the security of God's promises.
BV4637.S96   2011
234'.23—dc22   2011004704

ISBN 978-0-8007-4076-4 (casebound)

Published in association with the literary agency Fedd & Company, Inc., 606 Flamingo Blvd., Austin, TX 78734.

21 22 23 24 25 26 27   7 6 5 4 3 2 1

JJ, Joshua, Andrew, and Aster

Thank you for believing in me and this message, and for giving me time to write it. When my confidence wavered and my heart grew weary, God provided His strength *for me* and His confidence *in me* through you.

But blessed are those who trust in the LORD and have made the LORD their hope and confidence. (Jer. 17:7 NLT)

Contents

Contents

Foreword

As a little girl, I longed for a daddy to pick me up, swing me around, and tell me that I was special. That I was beautiful. That I was treasured. And most of all, that I was loved. But my daddy never swung me around with great delight, and he never said the words my heart desperately longed to hear. This rejection became an adult emptiness and brokenness that made me doubt I was lovable.

Insecurities cut deep. Shame ran rampant. Desperation for acceptance drove me to seek out all kinds of misguided remedies.

My primary remedy was to find someone or something that would make me feel secure and significant. It was as if I carried around a little heart-shaped cup and held it out to whatever or whomever I perceived might fill it.

I presented the cup to my education: "Will you fill me?"
I offered it to my husband: "Will you fill me?"
I held it out to my child: "Will you fill me?"
I extended it to my material possessions: "Will you fill me?"
I presented it to each of my jobs: "Will you fill me?"

Within this question were many more entanglements: "Will you right all my wrongs?" "Will you fill up my insecurities?" The more I offered my emptiness, hoping something could fill it, the more inadequate I felt.

Why do we look to things of this world to give us security, self confidence, and fulfillment?

I think it's because the message that worldly things can fulfill us is all around us. It's on TV, it's the focus of countless songs, and it dominates advertisements. We can't even stand in the grocery store checkout lane without being bombarded by empty promises for a more fulfilling life. A better husband. A better body. A better career. A more beautifully decorated house. The magazines seem so slick, their promises so enticing. They sneak into our thought processes and make us think, *If only I had _____, I'd be so secure and fulfilled.*

But the reality is, every single thing the world offers is temporary. No person, possession, profession, or position can ever fill the cup of a wounded, insecure heart—not my heart, not your heart. It's an emptiness only God can fill. Only God can give true confidence.

And how does God give us the gift of His security, fulfillment and confidence? He sends His words like love letters from Heaven to fall fresh on our parched and tired souls.

His truth waters us, sustains us, breathes new life into us and remakes us into the women He always intended us to be.

That's why I'm so excited about Renee's book. She is the friend you will find at the heart of this message. She's walked this journey and gives us the gift of truths she's discovered that will sweep away self-doubt and usher in the godly confidence we've been longing for our whole lives. Read this book and get ready to live with a confident heart.

Lysa TerKeurst, president, Proverbs 31 Ministries;
New York Times bestselling author, *Made to Crave*

Acknowledgments

I've never had the opportunity to thank the people who have helped shape my life and my confidence—people who believed in me long before I believed in myself. I am so grateful to get to do that here. Some I've known all my life, others for several years, and still some I haven't even met in person. I'll do my best to say a lot in a little space, so this doesn't become the longest chapter of the book. And if my forty-something-year-old foggy brain forgets someone, please know I love you and thank God for you!

First to my husband and hero, JJ, you are an amazing man, husband, father, and friend. I don't know how I got chosen to be yours, but I'm so glad I did! Without your words of affirmation, your confidence in God's calling on my life, and your servant's heart, I'm not sure I'd have had the courage and perseverance to do this. Thank you for sacrificing so much because you love me, but more so because you love Jesus and desire that He be made famous through the message He's entrusted to us. I respect and love you more than words can say.

Joshua, your passion for reading and your gift of writing inspire me. But your thoughtfulness, perseverance, and wisdom blow me away and make me proud to be your mom. Thank you for your constant sacrifice and support during our year of "impossible." I pray your courage and strength will always be found in Christ, and that this message will become a legacy we live and leave together. I'll never forget the times you told me you'd do whatever I needed so that I could finish my book. I did it! Now it's your turn.

Andrew, God knew I needed more laughter and joy, so he gave me you! Your hugs, smile, encouragement, and the conversations you create to keep our family connected are such a gift! I love how you see God in everyday life and that you still let your mom in on the amazing journey of discovering who God created you to be. I value and respect who you are, and who you're becoming as you dig into God's Word and claim His promises for your life. May He alone be your confidence.

Aster, my Ethiopian princess. Never did I think I'd adopt a baby and write a book in the same year. Your momma is crazy, but not that crazy. Yet God's crazy, amazing love brought us together for such a time as this. I treasure your sweet hugs, contagious joy, and oh-so-kissable cheeks. From the first day I held you in my arms, Jesus has changed my life with your love. I cannot imagine a day without you! Sweetheart, you are already a beautiful display of His splendor, a royal diadem in the hand of your God. May your security and worth always be found in Him!

Mom, when I was sixteen you told me God must have a plan for my life. It was the night He spared my life from being lost in that horrible car accident. Your words painted a picture on the canvas of my heart that sent me searching for His purpose. I think this book might be part of it! Thank you for believing in me and loving me through it all. I'm grateful for the "kingdom" Jesus has given us to enjoy now in this new season of our lives.

Dad, Mark, Scott, Brad, Chris, Beth, Tamika, and Robin, thank you for your love, encouragement, and support!

Melanie and Leah, I couldn't have written or lived this message without you both by my side! Thanks for listening to me, laughing at me, carrying the weight of the world with me, and telling me I was "normal" even when it wasn't true (smiles). Your constant prayers and calming presence are God's gifts to me!

MaryAnn, who would I be without your prayers and friendship? Your unending gifts of encouragement, spiritual wisdom, and unconditional love have shaped my life. Your fingerprints are all over my heart and my story.

Lysa and Holly, thanks for your steadfast love, confidence, patience, and grace in the midst of the hardest holy thing I've ever done. Your lives and your love inspire me to become immeasurably more than I can think of or imagine.

LeAnn, you always know just what to say when I need you to say it. Thank you for making sure I don't take myself too seriously, but more than anything for loving me like Jesus does! I see Him in you every day.

To each of my Proverbs 31 Ministries sisters, you are my treasured friends and forever family! When I need to see or feel God's love, I can come to the office or pick up the phone, and it is well with my soul. I am honored to serve Jesus with you, and I wouldn't want to do life or ministry without you!

Bev, thank you for your smile that affirms me, your tears that tell me God is speaking through something I said, and the joyful enthusiasm you show every time you hear me teach. Boy, did He fill in my gaps with your help. I love and treasure you!

Alli, what would I have done without my leopard-print key to your townhouse that became my home away from home? Thanks for sharing your Oreos, Triscuits, and toilet paper—and anything else I needed. I love you and miss you so much!

My thanks to my faithful friends and extended family who carried my heart and my hopes in your prayers: Jen, Angela, Melissa N., Margaret, Angel, Karen, Vicki and Derwin, Fern and Jay, Teresa, Missy, Renee, Becky, Charlena, Debbie, Kim N., Vern, Cris, Tori, Nancy and Terry, Sara, Alex, Jason and Sharon, Rusty and Erin, Bev and Jim, Jennifer and Phil, Erika, Heather and Mark, and my whole Transformation Church family.

Esther and AJ, you are the answer to my impossible prayer! Thank you for your expertise, friendship, vision, and passion for my ministry and the message God had written on my heart. I'm so grateful for both of you!

Andrea Doering, my amazing executive editor and friend, you are one of a kind! My heart felt at home with you the first time we met. Thank you for believing in my dreams and carrying my message with such grace and eagerness.

To my wonderful publishing team at Revell, Janelle, Twila, Lindsey, Deonne, Michele, Rod, Rob, and the rest of the Baker-Revell family for all you have done and will do to bring this message to the hearts of those who long to live with confidence. Thank you for seeking Christ and His glory in all you do!

To my *Confident Heart* prayer team, a very special thank you, as well as my faithful blog and Facebook friends, amazing women's event leaders, and their ministry teams who so faithfully prayed and encouraged me through this journey!

Most of all, my sweet Jesus, thank You for not letting me throw away my confidence anymore. You encouraged me to persevere so that when I had done Your will, I would receive what You had promised! Because of Your life in me and my dependence on You, I found the confidence to believe and live in the assurance of Your love and the security of Your promises. You are my confidence!

Hebrews 10:35–36

1

Discovering the Shadow
of My Doubts

So do not throw away your confidence; it will be richly rewarded. You need to persevere so that when you have done
the will of God, you will receive what he has promised.

Hebrews 10:35–36

I stood in front of my bathroom mirror, squinting from the
bright lights above while also trying to open my eyelids so
I could brush mascara on my lashes. My mouth opened too,
almost instinctively. I couldn't help but wonder why opening
my mouth also opened my eyes. It didn't make sense and
neither did the way I was feeling.

My heart was wrestling with self-doubt regarding an event
I would be speaking at the next day. I had felt honored, confident, and excited when the leader called months before to
invite me to speak at their women's event. Now I questioned

whether I should have accepted the invitation in the first place. I couldn't help but wonder, *What's wrong with me?*

I needed to get ready, finish packing my suitcase, and drive to the airport. Instead, I wanted to stay home and do something predictable like fold laundry, order pizza, and watch a movie with my kids. Something less risky than standing in front of five hundred women to give a message that I hoped would challenge and encourage their hearts, bring them laughter, and leave them longing for more of God.

Questions replayed over and over in my head: *What if I completely forget what I am going to say? What if my points aren't that powerful? What if the women don't connect with my stories or laugh at my humor? What if . . . ?*

As I continued to put on my makeup, I asked God—once again—to please take away my uncertainty. I hated feeling this way. Canceling the event wasn't an option. Maybe I could call in sick? No, that wouldn't be good.

This was not the first time I'd struggled with self-doubt. In fact, doubt was something I had dealt with more times than I wanted to recount. As a child I doubted I was worth keeping. My insecurity even kept me from riding the carousel at an amusement park, because I doubted my dad would wait for me. I thought he might leave me forever once I was out of sight.

Doubt also robbed me of the joy of waterskiing as a young girl. I refused to try it because I wasn't sure my family would come back to get me once I let go of the rope. I questioned whether I was good enough in college, so I avoided some great opportunities because they brought the risk of rejection. Even as a young bride, I doubted my husband's faithfulness. Our newlywed memories include a lot of arguments about trust.

Now here I was years later, a grown woman in ministry, doubting myself again. It was getting old. I wondered if perhaps my self-doubt was a sign I was in the wrong calling. I mean, if God calls you to do something, shouldn't you feel confident about it? Shouldn't you want to do it? Shouldn't self-assurance be part of God's equipping?

Maybe you know exactly what I'm talking about. Perhaps you have prayed since you were a little girl to be a mother, and here you are with kids, doubting you have what it takes to be a good mom. Or maybe you've sensed God calling you to serve Him in a way that requires steps of faith, but insecurity has convinced you that you're not smart enough or gifted enough. Perhaps you have wanted to change jobs for a while and now you have the opportunity to do just that, but you don't want to go. The unknown is too scary. Although you've been miserable, at least the misery is familiar where you are now.

I desperately wanted to move out of the shadow of my doubts, but all I could do was go through the motions and pray that God would zap me with confidence. I kept hoping it would happen right there in my bathroom, but it didn't. Doubt and questions continued to criticize me.

Once I finished brushing on my mascara, I turned around to put my makeup bag in my suitcase, which was on the floor behind me. That's when I noticed a huge nine-foot shadow on the wall. I was surprised by how much bigger my shadow was than my five-foot-two-inch frame.

It was distorting my image on the wall by making my body look bigger than it really was. All of a sudden, it dawned on me. My uncertainty had created a huge shadow of doubt. Just like my shadow on the wall was distorting my shape, my doubt was distorting my thoughts and overpowering my emotions with confusion and questions. The shadow of doubt had become bigger than what I doubted—myself.

I just stood there looking at the humongous shadow. Then I bent down to put my makeup bag in my suitcase and sensed

God whispering to my heart: *You can only see the shadow because you have turned away from the light. Turn back toward the light.*

As I stood up and turned back toward the light above the mirror, I realized I was no longer standing in the shadow. And that was the day I discovered the shadow of my doubts.

Listening to Doubt's Whispers

In the shadow of doubt, insecurity paralyzes us with statements like:

"I can't do this."
"Things will never change."
"My life isn't going to get better."
"I'll never have the confidence I need."

Those are some depressing thoughts, aren't they? But oh how quickly they weasel their way into our minds and disguise their voices to sound like ours. Sometimes we agree with them and they become our own.

These are the voices of insecurity that cast shadows of doubt over our perspective and keep us from becoming the women we want to be—the women God created us to be. Self-doubt blocks the promise of God's power and truth to change us from the inside out so that we can live with a confident heart.

Have you ever agreed with the whispers of doubt and found yourself living with a sense of discouragement and defeat? Have you felt paralyzed by insecurity, and let it stop you from living confidently? If so, you are not alone.

Maybe, like me, you have wondered why you struggle with self-doubt. Or maybe you've asked God to take away your insecurities and give you a more confident personality, yet you are still waiting for that to happen. Perhaps you are good at hiding your doubts and no one but you knows the paralyzing power they have on your life.

As you read the title of this book, did any hint of doubt creep in to tell you it's not possible to have a confident heart? It wouldn't surprise me. Doubt keeps us from believing things can get better. Doubt convinces us that it's not worth the effort. Doubt shouts from the sidelines:

"It's too hard."

"You might as well quit."

"Go ahead and give up. Just close the book now and walk away."

It's Not Supposed to Be This Way

Don't listen to those thoughts, my friend. God doesn't want us stuck in a cycle of defeat or living in the shadows of doubt. He reminds us in Isaiah 49:23, "Then you will know that I am the LORD. Those who hope in me will not be disappointed." Yet, doubt and hope cannot live in our hearts at the same time. As God's girls, we need to know and believe that change is possible. We need to hope that life can be different. Otherwise, doubt will win every time and our hearts will be eroded by attitudes and emotions of defeat—but it is not supposed to be this way.

God declares with confidence that things can change— "See, I am doing a new thing!" "I am working all things together for good, because you love me and are called according to my purpose." "All things are possible to [her] who believes" (Isa. 43:19; Rom. 8:28; Mark 9:23 NASB).

Over the past few years, I've found lasting confidence by living daily in the security of God's promises. He's led me beyond believing *in Him* to really *believing Him* by relying on the power of His words and living like they are true no matter what my feelings tell me. Some days I do better than others, and you will too. But I've found that when I choose to dwell in the assurance of Whose I am and who I am in Him, I have a confident heart.

The God of all hope is calling you out of the shadow of your doubts so you can live with a confident heart! Are you ready to let His Word change the way you think, which will determine the way you feel and eventually transform the way you live (Rom. 12:2)? This will be a process that happens if you are willing to have honest, soul-searching conversations with God, yourself, and a few people you trust—conversations about where you are, how you got here, and where you really long to be.

If you are looking for a friend you can trust with the things of your heart, this book is a great place to start. I promise to create honest conversations about our doubts that will challenge us to live beyond them. We'll look back so we can move forward, and talk about how we got to this place of being so hard on ourselves.

We'll do the most important thing first: spend time digging deep into the heart and character of God so we can learn to depend on His heart toward us. The next three chapters will be foundational as we examine and grow in our understanding of who God is and who we are to Him. We will take the first steps out of the shadows of doubt as we choose to embrace the reality of His measureless grace, unconditional love, and redeeming hope.

Next, we'll identify the triggers of our self-doubt and the destructive effects they have on our lives and relationships. We'll learn how to live beyond the shadows of doubt by holding each of our insecurities up to the light of God's

Word. We'll talk about the struggles, uncertainties, and fears we all face and how we can learn to actively trust God's heart as we process our never-ending thoughts, our always-changing emotions, and our oh-so-busy and often confusing lives through the transforming truth of God's Word. We will find our heart's confidence in Christ as we learn how to rely on the power of His promises in our everyday lives.

Before we get started, there are a few things I want to make sure you don't miss. At the end of each chapter I have included something really important: a prayer that weaves together Scriptures we've talked about in the chapter and others I want us to engrave on our hearts. Praying God's Word has been one of the most life-changing ways I've learned to live in the security of His promises.

One way God tells us that confidence will come is when we ask Him for what is already part of His will. "This is the confidence which we have before Him, that, if we ask anything according to His will, He hears us" (1 John 5:14 NASB). So there you go: we can be confident we are praying God's will when we pray God's Word!

But that's not all. Romans 10:17 tells us that "faith comes from hearing, and hearing by the word of Christ" (NASB), so let's pray these promises out loud again and again. That might seem weird but trust me, it works. When we pray God's words out loud, and hear them, the Holy Spirit engraves them on our hearts and writes them in our thoughts. We internalize God's truth as our faith grows and we are transformed from the inside out!

I also hope you will take time to answer the reflection and discussion questions after the prayer in each chapter. These will be an essential part of processing, internalizing, and applying God's promises to your life. Be sure to get a journal or notebook to write out the promise prayers and your answers to the questions so you can look back and see what God has done.

Reading this with a small group of friends would be ideal, but if you are going through it on your own, that's great too. I've created a section of my interactive website where I would love for you to be part of the conversation with me and other women who are seeking to live with confident hearts. I'd love to hear your thoughts and your story at www.ReneeSwope .com as we take this journey together.

Are you ready to take God's hand and trust His heart? If so, let's get started together in prayer.

Praying God's Promises

Lord, I pray that You would give me a confident heart in Christ. Take me beyond believing in You to truly believing You. Help me rely on the power of Your promises and live like they are true. You say blessed is the one who trusts in You and whose hope and confidence are found in You. Those who hope in You will not be disappointed, because You work all things together for good for those who love You and are called according to Your purpose.

When self-doubt tells me I can't overcome my insecurities, I will believe Your promise that all things are possible to whoever believes. I will not throw away my confidence, because You say it will be richly rewarded. I will persevere so that when I have done the will of God, I will receive what You have promised. My confidence is in Christ and I am no longer one who shrinks back and is destroyed, but one who believes and is saved! In Jesus' name, Amen.

See Jeremiah 17:7; Isaiah 49:23; Romans 8:28; Mark 9:23; Hebrews 10:35–36, 39.

Reflection and Discussion Questions

1. What is your earliest memory of doubting yourself or feeling insecure?
2. Has insecurity ever kept you from doing something?
3. Describe how it makes you feel when doubt whispers:
   "I can't do this."
   "Things will never change."
   "My life isn't going to get better."
   "It's too hard."
   "I might as well quit."
4. Describe what happens in your heart when you read God's words:
   "Those who hope in me will not be disappointed" (Isa. 49:23).
   "See, I am doing a new thing!" (Isa. 43:19).
   "And we know that in all things God works for the good of those who love him, who have been called according to his purpose" (Rom. 8:28).
   "All things are possible to [her] who believes" (Mark 9:23 NASB).
5. What do you think hinders you most from living with God-confidence on a consistent basis? Is there a promise listed above that speaks to your greatest need right now?
6. How would you describe a woman with a confident heart?
7. Read Jeremiah 17:7. What does this verse promise and encourage you to do? Think of one situation where you could live in the power of this promise and describe what that would look like this week.

2

Because God's Love Is Perfect, I Don't Have to Be

It is a rare soul indeed who has been sought after for who she is—not because of what she can do, or what others can gain from her, but simply for herself . . . so what are we to conclude? Often we conclude that there is nothing in our hearts worth knowing. Whoever and whatever this mystery called *I* must be, it cannot be much.

John Eldredge and Brent Curtis[1]

As I pulled into my driveway, I noticed an envelope taped to our front door. Immediately I tried to remember what I had done to deserve a thank-you note, but couldn't think of anything. I was so excited I didn't even open our garage door. Instead I parked in the driveway, hopped out of my car, and walked to the porch to get my note.

Much to my dismay, I discovered it was not a thank-you note. Instead, it was a notice. Someone on the neighborhood architectural committee had stopped by to inform us that our windowsills and front porch columns needed to be repaired and painted within thirty days, or we'd be fined. I was humiliated!

Did our house look bad enough to warrant an official notice? Had they taken the time to peek through the windows and see our new floors and kitchen renovations? I defended myself to the "neighborhood police," who weren't even there to listen. I imagined them sitting around a table, talking about us in a homeowners' meeting while writing other citations for excessive yard debris and inappropriate paint colors.

My humiliation turned to frustration when my husband got home a few minutes later. He didn't know what to think as I wagged the envelope in my hand and told him, "There are four hundred homes in our neighborhood, and plenty of them are in much worse condition. How could they even see our windowsills and front porch? There is at least forty feet between our house and the curb."

We had huge Bradford pear trees in our yard that blocked the view from the street so I knew someone must have come onto our property. To prove my point, I marched to the street and announced that I could barely see the windows or columns. "Our house looks fine," I insisted.

It really did—from a distance. But as I walked back up to the porch and looked more closely, I had to admit that the winter winds and summer heat had worn the paint thin. It was peeling in a few places and the wood on our thirty-foot columns needed some repair. Since we had spent months (and most of our money) replacing countertops, floors, and carpets inside, we started making plans to complete the outside work ourselves. What we thought would take a few hours turned into several days. We spent weekends on ladders scraping, sanding, priming, and painting.

From a Distance

The more we sanded and scraped, the more the paint peeled. As I painted, I thought about how our house really did look fine from a distance. Then I thought about how much I can be just like my house. From a distance, I look like I'm doing just fine.

It can be hard to let people know how we're really doing. We don't want to be high maintenance, right? We surely don't want people to see the peeling paint of our imperfections or the rotting attitudes in the wood boards of our minds. It's embarrassing for people to see our flaws and failures, so we work hard to look like we're doing fine from a distance.

Sometimes I think we tell people we're fine even when we're not, because we want to be fine. Or we hope that by saying we are fine, eventually we will be. Other times we act like we're fine because others expect us to be. Of course, there are days when hormones trump all good manners and reason. Days when anyone within ten feet knows you are not fine. Although we tell people we're fine, what we really mean is that we are Frazzled, Irritated, Neurotic, and Exhausted!

Being honest about who we are and how we are doing is especially risky when it comes to our insecurities. We fear that if people know we doubt ourselves, they'll start doubting us too. We walk into work on Monday morning with a smile, hoping no one will ask about our weekend. The sting of rejection is still raw after not being invited to a coworker's barbecue when everyone else was. Or we pull up in the carpool line, and someone asks about Christmas. "It was fine," we say, holding back the tears that follow a holiday filled with pain, strife, loneliness, and disappointment.

Sunday morning is the worst. How many of us rush out the door, fuss about what our kids are wearing and how they are acting, drive to church arguing with our husband, and then tell ourselves we're the worst mom and wife on the planet? We're convinced if anyone found out who we really are they wouldn't let us into church. Then we walk into the service—smiling. Someone asks how we're doing and we lie through our teeth: "I'm fine! We're doing great!"

Pretending

Pretending leads to hiding and isolation. What we need is someone who will pursue us and accept us even though we're flawed. Yet most of us doubt anyone would ever stick with us if we let them get too close. So we put up walls and hide our struggles, even from God, hoping we'll convince Him and everyone else that we're fine.

Eventually, though, we find ourselves in the shadows of doubt, convinced that we aren't worth knowing or pursuing. Slowly we begin to believe we have to be perfect to be loved and accepted. We know we never will be—but we'll die trying, won't we?

For much of my life, I put expectations of perfection on myself because I thought if I let others see my weaknesses and insecurities they would think less of me—and eventually leave me. My parents divorced when I was two, and my dad remarried. Although we spent time together and he would often give me things, it was hard for him to give much of himself.

Yet I longed for my father's love and approval. I thought if I could only make good grades, be prettier or smarter, accomplish things, or get the kind of degree he wanted me to get, then my daddy would value me. As an adult, I have come to realize that I believed I wasn't worth staying for, and if I had only done something differently my father would not have left us.

"You're not worth staying for" was a lie, but it became the truth through which I filtered my worth in all of my relationships. I tried to earn my worth through a performance-based value system, convinced that if I did the right things, said the right things, wore the right things, and looked the right way, then I'd be worth staying for.

My life was far from perfect, but I didn't want anyone to know. On the outside everything looked "fine," yet on the inside I was haunted by thoughts of never being good enough. I felt like I could never do enough to measure up.

Oh how I longed for someone to see past the exterior façade and look into the secret places of my heart. I wanted to be known and loved for who I was. Yet if I let my guard down, I was afraid someone would say I was too sensitive or too serious. It had happened before. So I pretended everything was fine. With each attempt to keep others impressed and distant, I stepped further into the shadows of doubt. Even though I was surrounded by people, my insecurities convinced me I was all alone.

By the time I was in college, I couldn't pretend anymore. I ran out of paint. The columns of my life started to crumble. The sills around the windows of my heart began to rot.

Although I had been going to church off and on for years, I had never really understood the messages I heard. I went to church because my friends were going. I went because my boyfriend invited me, which meant I'd get to spend more time with him on Sunday. Finally, in my early twenties, I started going for me. I started listening and truly hearing what was being said.

One day I realized I couldn't keep pretending. I was not fine, and I couldn't fake it anymore.

Up Close and Personal

Slowly but surely, the walls around my heart started to come down. Over time God revealed His heart to me through sermons at a nearby church and books I read, but more than anything He spoke to me through the Bible. Through His written Word on the page and His living Word in the person of Christ, I came to know an up close and personal Savior who pursues imperfect women like me. I read stories that echoed the struggles and desires of my heart. Tucked within those stories I discovered God's promises and how He responds to the longings and hurts of His children. I read words that gave me hope and assured me that I was not alone.

One of my favorite pictures of God's pursuit of us is in the Gospel of John, chapter 4. The story's main character is referred to as the Samaritan woman, but I like to call her Sam. It makes her feel more like the real woman she was, with a heart that had been broken just like so many of ours. Sam had searched for years to find acceptance, love, and approval in the heart of a man.

She'd been married five times. In her culture women could not divorce their husbands, so she had been discarded by five men and was now living with a man who didn't think she was worth committing to. We meet her one day while she is running errands and running away from those who knew all about her flaws and failed marriages. Feeling imperfect and ashamed, she walked to the well alone that day.

Typically, women came to the well in the morning or early evening. They traveled together in the cool of the day, avoiding the scorching heat of the sun since they would be carrying heavy jars filled with water back to their homes. But not Sam; she walked there all by herself.

Many theologians believe that instead of avoiding the scorching heat of the sun, she went to the well at noon to avoid the scorching pain of others' rejection and judgment. The weight of the water-filled jar in the heat must have been almost unbearable, but the weight of her neighbors' words, reminding her of her failures and imperfections, was more than she could take.

I imagine at one time Sam had walked to the well with the other women from her small town. They would talk about their day, their husbands, and their kids—but then they started talking about her. Whispers and condescending glances must have come after her first divorce, judgment and shame after her second. At what point had Sam distanced herself? Had she made excuses to stay back while the other women went ahead, insisting she was "fine," but would go later? Let's pick up her story where she meets Jesus:

> When a Samaritan woman came to draw water, Jesus said to her, "Will you give me a drink?" . . .
>
> The Samaritan woman said to him, "You are a Jew and I am a Samaritan woman. How can you ask me for a drink?" (For Jews do not associate with Samaritans.)
>
> Jesus answered her, "If you knew the gift of God and who it is that asks you for a drink, you would have asked him and he would have given you living water." (John 4:7–10)

When Sam saw Jesus sitting at the well that day, she didn't know who He was. She could tell by the way He was dressed that He was Jewish and wondered why He was talking to her, a Samaritan. Men didn't talk to women in public places. Sam must have avoided eye contact at first. Did she wonder if

He wanted something, like all the other men in her life? He did—but it wasn't what she must have expected.

When He spoke, she heard gentleness in His voice. There was kindness and humility in His simple request for a drink. When she looked into His eyes she saw acceptance, not judgment; love, not hate. She felt valuable in His presence, as though she had something to offer. There was something different about Him.

He Is There

Jesus could have chosen to be anywhere else that day, but instead He was there pursuing Sam. John tells us in verse 4 that Jesus "*had* to go through Samaria." Jews considered Samaritans to be the scum of the earth. Usually if they were near Samaria they would travel around it—but not Jesus. He *had* to go through Samaria, because He knew Sam would be there.

Knowing she was running from the very thing that reminded her of her imperfections, Jesus timed it so that she would run into Him and find perfect love. He initiated conversation and asked her for the one thing she had to offer: water. It wasn't much, but it was a starting point. Sam could have easily filled her jar and headed back home, returning to her busy day. But she stopped and listened.

Jesus met Sam in one of the loneliest parts of her day. In the same way, He is there waiting for us in the midst of our imperfect lives, when our pain and failures confirm our self-doubts. He is there waiting for us when we're going through the motions, aware of what needs to be done but unaware of how we're going to do it. He is there on those mornings when we can't stop criticizing ourselves for blowing it the day before; when we go to work and wonder why we're even there.

During endless days filled with changing diapers and doing laundry, wondering if we'll ever find meaning in the monotony of motherhood, He is there. When we come home to an empty house and wonder why we don't have a family, or come home to a teenager who belittles us and a husband who ignores us, Jesus is there.

If you've ever doubted God's personal pursuit of you, let this truth sink in, my friend: wherever you are, He wants to meet you there. He is waiting for you to stop, come up close, and turn your heart to listen to His. You don't have to pretend things are fine when they aren't. He knows what is going on in your thoughts. Nothing could keep Him from wanting to be with you.

He invites you to come to Him to receive the perfect love He offers—love that casts out fear, love that is patient and kind, love that keeps no record of wrongs. That is what He offered Sam, and it's what He offers you and me.

Will This Make My Life Easier?

Jesus told Sam if she knew who she was talking to, she wouldn't even bother with the water in the well. Instead, she would ask Him for life-giving water:

> Jesus answered, "Everyone who drinks this water will be thirsty again, but whoever drinks the water I give them will never thirst. Indeed, the water I give them will become in them a spring of water welling up to eternal life."
>
> The woman said to him, "Sir, give me this water so that I won't get thirsty and have to keep coming here to draw water." (John 4:11–15)

Sam didn't understand the fullness of His promise, so she focused on the first part of Jesus' sentence, which equated in her mind to "this could make my life easier." Never thirsting again meant she wouldn't have to come back to the well every day. Her errands would be shorter and her to-do list cut in half!

Do you ever read God's promises and fall into the pattern of thinking, "Oh, it would make my life so much easier if God would just do this"? I do. It's easy to approach God like a magic genie, hoping He'll grant our wishes. Some days I'll tell God what I need to get done and minimize my prayers to asking Him to bless my efforts.

Now I'm not implying that God isn't concerned with our daily needs; He cares about every detail in our lives. But if we only live on the surface with God, we'll never experience the intimacy we long for or the acceptance and security He offers.

Instead of just making our lives easier, God wants us to come up close and experience Him and all that He has for us. He knows that our problems won't be solved and our confidence won't be found through simply getting more stuff done.

Instead, He invites us to slow down and talk to Him about our day and the desires of our hearts, asking Him to show us the reasons for our doubts and insecurities. He wants us to go below the surface by asking Him to show us *why* we want what we want. Then we can ask Him if what we want is really what we need.

Below the Surface

Sam wanted Jesus to change the course of her day, but she needed Him to change the course of her life. Much like the path she wore back and forth to this well each day to draw water, there was a path she wore back and forth to the hearts of men, hoping they could quench her emotional thirst.

Jesus knew Sam, like us, longed to be loved and pursued for who she was—not for what she could do but simply for herself. The only way He could satisfy the thirst of her soul was to help her see it. He could offer her living water, but first she had to want it, ask for it, and then receive it. And so Jesus took their conversation below the surface:

> He told her, "Go, call your husband and come back."
>
> "I have no husband," she replied.
>
> Jesus said to her, "You are right when you say you have no husband. The fact is, you have had five husbands, and the man you now have is not your husband. What you have just said is quite true." (John 4:16–18)

Can you imagine Sam's pain? I feel the emptiness in her confession: "I have no husband." It must have been so hard to say those words, knowing she had had five husbands, and then to discover this man already knew so much about her. She had been rejected and abandoned five times.

Sam was uncomfortable and didn't want to go below the surface, so she quickly changed the subject.

> "Sir," the woman said, "I can see that you are a prophet. Our fathers worshiped on this mountain, but you Jews claim that the place where we must worship is in Jerusalem." (John 4:19–20)

Only a prophet could know so much about her, so she asked Him where she should go to church. I wonder if it was her way of saying, "Yes I've had five husbands, and I'm living with someone who won't commit. But it's no big deal, I'm fine." Or was it an attempt to cover her sin with good deeds? Was she saying, "My personal life is in shambles, but I'm a good person. I want to do good things. So tell me, where should I go to church, on this mountain or in Jerusalem?"

Have you ever put on a façade that everything was okay when it wasn't? Have you ever been afraid to let people know who you really are? Wouldn't you love to be in such a safe place that you could stop pretending and be real with God and yourself (and eventually other people) about where you are and how you got there?

Jesus asked Sam these questions so she would see the pattern of her life and what it was doing to her. He took her below the surface and showed her what was really going on in her heart. He helped Sam see that each broken relationship had convinced her she was not worth staying for.

In the same way, Jesus wants to help you see what is going on in your heart and what you are struggling with that is eroding your security and confidence. If you were sitting with Jesus today, what do you think He'd want to talk about? Perhaps your heart needs to be set free from pretending and perfectionism. Are you longing for others' approval and wonder why you can never get enough?

Maybe you have experienced the pain of divorce or the devastation of a broken engagement. Have you found yourself in a cycle of unhealthy and destructive relationships and don't know why? Maybe insecurity or infidelity has caused you to doubt that someone better will ever come along. Maybe you don't even know what you're struggling with, and that is okay. Jesus does.

So many times we go through the motions, doing the same things over and over again, hoping something will change. Few of us realize that this repetition is the definition of insanity. Let's not look back and wish we'd done things differently. Let's go beneath the surface with Jesus so He can show us places in our hearts that need His repair.

To Be Known Is to Be Loved

Jesus knew Sam's story and He knows yours. The Hebrew word for "know" is *yada*. It means a deep emotional experience; a bonding between two people when one truly feels the emotions of the other. Jesus knows your pain, fears, doubts, and disappointments. He understands your dreams and desires.

Although some of us feel uncomfortable that God knows so much about us, it is good to be known, to be listened to and not judged. Jesus is the only One who can meet our deepest needs to be accepted and delighted in simply because of who we are. We can offer nothing but our presence, and He will desire us just the same.

Remember when Jesus told Sam that living water would become a spring in her, welling up to *eternal life*? I used to just skim over the words "eternal life" because they sounded so religious. I knew it meant Sam would get to be with Jesus for eternity, but I didn't see how that impacted my everyday life. However, one day God showed me why "eternal life" was such a crucial part of His promise to Sam and to us. In John 17:3, Jesus said, "This is eternal life: that they *know* you, the only true God, and Jesus Christ, whom you have sent" (emphasis added).

By offering Sam eternal life, Jesus was offering her the gift of His Holy Spirit, who would cleanse her sins. But even more than that, it would lead her into a relationship where she could *know* the one true God and be known by Him.

Why is that significant? Because Christianity is the only faith that offers a relationship with the living God. We don't just know *about* our God; our God wants us to *know* Him. We were created for that kind of relationship. He wants us to find lasting soul-security in knowing we are valued and pursued by the One who knows and loves us—the One who created our inmost being and wove us together in our mother's womb (Ps. 139:13). Have you let the gospel of God's grace move from your head to your heart, so that you know without a doubt you are known intimately and loved completely by God?

Our Image of God

I didn't grow up knowing about God's love. I didn't really know God for who He is, and I had no idea He wanted a personal relationship with me. Oftentimes our image of God is shaped by early childhood memories and perceptions, good and bad.

When I was a kid, I perceived God as distant, unavailable, and unapproachable. My image of Him conjured up feelings of fear and judgment instead of protection and acceptance. I wanted to please Him so He wouldn't get mad at me. I pictured Him on the sidelines of life, keeping score, and I felt like I was always disappointing Him. In a nutshell, I had created God in the image of my father.

My dad showed love by buying me things. So, if God brought good things in my life, I felt His approval. My dad showed disappointment through withdrawal and anger. When life was hard and I was lonely, I wondered what I had done wrong and if God was turning His back on me.

When I was twelve years old, my mom remarried and we moved to a small town in North Carolina. When you live in the Bible Belt, going to church every Sunday is like going to the swimming pool on hot summer days. It's just what you do, so I did.

That is when I started hearing about God's grace, love, and forgiveness. I heard how Jesus died for our sins and wants a relationship with us. Over time I came to know God for who He is through the person of Jesus Christ, who is "the radiance of God's glory and the exact representation of his being" (Heb. 1:3).

I discovered that God was not created in my father's image, but that as God's child I was created in His image instead. I was made to know Him and be known by Him—and so are you. Are there images of God in your heart that need to be replaced, repaired, or restored?

More Than Knowing

A personal relationship with God sets us free to be all we were created to be. As children of God we were designed to find our identity, our significance, and our confidence in Him. When we respond to God's invitation and accept Jesus' gift of salvation, we don't just accept a new philosophy of life. We establish a personal relationship with our Creator, the One who knows us and accepts us fully, but who also desires our transformation so we can become all He created us to be.

Remember back to the day I was painting our house? As I stood on the ladder, I thought about how badly the repairs were needed after all. I was no longer mad that someone in our neighborhood had come up close and gotten very personal. Instead, I was glad they cared enough to notice and tell us.

So it is with Jesus. He notices and cares enough to tell us that our hearts need repair. He won't leave a notice on our front door, but He did leave Himself as a love letter nailed to the cross of Calvary, declaring the depth of His perfect love. Through His death and resurrection, we are offered the gift of new life through the Holy Spirit and lasting security through our relationship with Christ.

The only way we'll have a confident heart is if we move beyond knowing about God to knowing and relying on Him—to depending on His Word with our whole heart, mind, and soul.

Maybe you are like me; you have believed in Him for years—but you haven't really *believed* Him completely. At least you don't always feel or live like His promises are true for you. Maybe you know God loves you and forgives you, but you still beat yourself up for mistakes you've made and the ways you think you've let Him and others down.

Today can be the day the gospel of grace moves from your head to your heart. Today can be the day you take your first steps out of the shadows of doubt and start really living in the truth.

Will you let your desire to be known and loved just as you are lead you into a more personal and intimate relationship with Jesus? The first step is to embrace your imperfections in the light of God's perfect love, "being confident of this, that he who began a good work in you will carry it on to completion until the day of Christ Jesus" (Phil. 1:6).

I also know it's possible that you are in a different place. A new place. An unknown place. Like Sam, maybe you know about God but you don't personally know God. I am so glad you have made it to this point and that you are taking this journey with me. I can only imagine how God is smiling now. I know how much He wants to give you His grace and truth. He's also inviting you into an up close and personal relationship through Jesus so that you can know Him, be set free through His forgiveness, and experience the fullness of His love.

If you would like to accept Jesus as Lord of your life, you can pray the following prayer or use it as a guide to create your own. Just talk to God from your heart, with honesty and sincerity.

Lord, I am sorry that I have done things to separate myself from You and other people. I confess I have sinned against You and ask You to forgive me. I acknowledge that I could never earn salvation by my good works, but I come to You and put my trust in what Jesus did for me on the cross. I believe You love me and that Jesus died and rose again so that I can be forgiven and come to know You. Come into my heart and be Lord of my life. I trust You and thank You for loving me so much that I can know You up close and personal here on earth, and spend the rest of eternity with You in heaven. In Jesus' name, Amen.

Sweet friend, wherever you are, Jesus meets you there. You and I are not worthy of His love and we can never do anything to deserve it—but we are worth His love because He chose to give it to us. We are His! Hold on to this promise and live in the power of its truth: because God's love is perfect, you don't have to be!

Praying God's Promises

May the God of our Lord Jesus Christ, the glorious Father, give me the Spirit of wisdom and revelation so that I may know Him better. I want to know and rely on the love You have for me, Jesus, and live in that love. You say that whoever lives in love lives in You, and You in him. In this way, love is made complete in me, so that I can have confidence today and forever. I want an up close and personal relationship with You, one where I don't have to pretend or hide.

When I feel insecure, insignificant, or unloved, remind me of Your perfect love that has the power to cast out my fear. Thank You for Your love that is patient, is kind, and keeps no record of my wrongs. I trust that because Your love is perfect, I don't have to be. I will remain in Your love and be confident of this: that He who began a good work in me will carry it on to completion until the day of Christ Jesus. In Jesus' name I pray, Amen.

See Ephesians 1:17; Hebrews 1:3; 1 John 4:16–18; 1 Corinthians 13:4–5; John 15:9; Philippians 1:6.

Reflection and Discussion Questions

1. Think back to your childhood and your first memory of God. Describe your image of Him growing up.

2. How does your childhood perception of God compare to what you see in Christ through His interaction with Sam? List the similarities and differences.

3. Do you ever feel like you are the only one who struggles with insecurity or doubt? Why or why not?

4. Jesus wants to create a safe place for you to be transparent with Him where you can ask questions and be real about your desires, doubts, disappointments, and dreams. He knows you and wants you to really know Him. Is the thought of this kind of relationship with God comforting or uncomfortable, and why?

5. Has anything ever happened that caused you to distance yourself from God or other people? How does it make you feel to know Jesus understands, and He is still there with you in every moment of every day? When do you need His assurance and presence most?

6. Reread Sam's story in John 4, asking Jesus to meet you there and show you things in your heart that need His repair. Is there part of my story or Sam's story that you relate to most?

7. What lesson from this chapter will you walk away with and hold on to so that you can live in the security of God's approval and acceptance?

3

Finding Love That Won't Fail
Even When I Do

How priceless is your unfailing love, O God! People take
refuge in the shadow of your wings.

Psalm 36:7

One Sunday afternoon I was feeling a little lost, in between my new life with Christ and my old life without
Him. It was the last semester of my senior year at Meredith
College, and there was something in my heart I just couldn't
settle. I had felt empty and confused for so much of my life,
and I couldn't figure out why all the relationships and things
I had worked so hard for couldn't fill me or fulfill me.

I decided to go for a walk under the canopy of oak trees
lining the road that encircled campus. Pressing my hands
into my pockets, I pulled my jacket tight, breathed in the

fresh air, and lifted my face toward the blue sky. The smell of azaleas and a cool breeze contrasted with the warmth of the sun against my cheeks and made me wonder how I could live in such a beautiful place for four years and still feel so empty and unhappy.

Life looked great on the outside: I was about to graduate with honors and had job offers, a new boyfriend, and a cute sports car. But on the inside I was dying a slow and lonely emotional death that my doctor had diagnosed as clinical depression. I thought about how I had filled my schedule and my mind with activities and responsibilities to the point of overload. I was hoping they would distract me from my emptiness.

When overcommitment didn't work, I tried to drink my way out of the pain. But my escape from the darkness into a place of temporary happiness would usually wear off by the next morning. My efforts to dig my way out of the pit were more like a shovel that dug a deeper hole for my heart to dwell in, a hollow place in my soul where feelings of hopelessness held me hostage. The more I did and the more I had, the more I questioned why I wasn't satisfied—and the more I doubted that I ever would be.

The Things We Do for Love

As I walked that day, my eyes drifted to the buildings, dorms, and other landmarks of my memories. Suddenly my mind was filled with a collage of faces, reminding me of my efforts and the people I had hoped could fill my emptiness. Seeing the admissions building made me think about my mom and how much she wanted me to go to Meredith College.

It wasn't a school we could afford. I had needed loans, scholarships, and grants. My stepfather insisted I could never go there, which made Mom even more determined that I would. The day she and I pulled up under the arch of welcome balloons, parked in front of the admissions building, and went through freshman check-in was my first day ever to set foot on campus.

I wanted to make my mom happy, so I agreed to move in with people I had never met and attend a college I had never visited in a city I had never been to. I tried hard to be excited the day we arrived, but instead a flood of tears threatened to break the dam of my emotions, held back by my fake smile.

Home was hours away, and so was my boyfriend. *What was I doing here?* I didn't know who I was or what I wanted. All my life I had depended on my mom to help me find out, but she had to go back home. When she left I was alone. Without her presence and guidance I felt lost.

As I continued to walk, I glanced at the amphitheater, across the street from the admissions building, where my graduation would be held in a few weeks. It was surrounded by beautiful green lawns where students would study and couples would cuddle on picnic blankets. I had been one of them.

Tears streamed down my face as I thought about my first love, the guy I dated all through high school and college. During the summer before my senior year, our plans of a future together crumbled under the pressure of me expecting him to be all that I needed, and him wanting freedom to be who he wanted. I had been crazy about him—a little too crazy.

I stood there thinking about the crazy things I did for his love. It makes me want to crawl under a rock when I think about them today. Although I had driven him away, I wanted him to want me back. I wanted him to tell me I was worth what it would take to change so we could be happy together. In passing, one day, a friend mentioned that my ex-boyfriend was heading to our hometown for the weekend. We worked near each other, so I decided to park by his office and wait for him to leave on Friday.

We both "happened" to be at Wendy's getting dinner at the same time and bumped into each other. He offered his puppy-dog smile, which only made me more desperate. When I finished my order, I got in my car just in time to pull out and follow behind him for hours, because I "happened" to be going home for the weekend too.

All the while I was hoping he'd slow down and signal for me to pull over so we could talk. I was hoping that seeing me at Wendy's and the reflection of my car in his rearview mirror had brought him to the realization that he just couldn't live without me.

Seriously, what was I thinking? As you can probably guess, he never pulled over and told me I was worth what it would take to make our love last. That summer, something in me broke. When he told me he couldn't be what I needed him to be, I heard, "You're not worth as much as the beer and partying you want me to give up."

I tried to escape my old feelings of abandonment and to silence insecurity's curse that whispered: "See, you're *not* worth staying for." To numb my pain, I started doing what I had begged him to stop doing; I drank excessive amounts of alcohol every day. Without his love, I felt incomplete.

All I Ever Wanted

Standing there, looking at the amphitheater, I wiped the tears from my eyes and the memories from my mind and started walking again. With each passing building I thought of teachers, advisers, friends, and counselors who tried to help me figure out what was wrong. Although I had achieved success,

I felt like a failure. They would remind me of all I had accomplished and the future I had ahead of me.

That would make me feel better for a little while, but then I'd slip back into the familiar place of self-doubt. I felt like such a disappointment to them and myself. My mom had raised me to be a determined and strong woman. She had sent me to college to get a good education so I would never have to depend on anyone. According to everyone's standards, that is what I should have been at this point: a confident woman. But my heart felt like a shoreline that had been washed away by the tides of broken relationships, insecurities, and shattered dreams.

I stopped walking again and just stood there, taking it all in. I couldn't help but wonder, *Why was it never enough? Why was all that I had never enough to fill me and fulfill me?*

I don't remember if I was talking to God or to myself, but I have no doubt that He answered. A thought rushed through my soul, stringing together two words I had never put next to each other in a sentence.

Renee, all you have ever wanted is unconditional love.

Unconditional love? I didn't know there was such a thing. I doubted there could be. Then I heard a whisper in my soul that spoke to my heart with such clarity I knew it wasn't me talking. *You've been trying to earn your value in everything you've done. But you will never find the love you long for in anyone or anything but Me. I AM the unconditional love you are looking for.*

Unconditional love. Two words I had never put together became the answer to my life's question. In my mind these words were antonyms. I had no concept of love without conditions. It was all I had ever known. The thought of God valuing me so much that His love would never fail—even if I failed Him—was inconceivable, yet something deep in my soul told me it was true. I had been looking for love that could not be taken away. Love that wouldn't fail, even when I did. Love I didn't have to earn. Love I could never lose. I didn't know what to do.

Searching for Significance

Looking back, now I can see I had been searching for significance and trying to fill an empty place in my heart with people, places, and things. I had been trying to earn my parents' approval because I lived for their affirmation. I worked hard to prove my worth and value to my professors and friends, but it was never enough. Until our hearts find complete security and significance in God's unconditional love, we will never be satisfied.

Those of us who struggle with insecurity and find ourselves in the shadow of doubt often get there because we are seeking our validation in people's opinions, our worth in accomplishments, and our identity in excessive commitments. It can only go on for so long before something breaks. We either get tired and quit trying, or we push ourselves to the point of burnout because we don't know how to set boundaries.

That was me. I always had to be *doing* something. I still have to be careful, but we'll talk more about that later. My unhealthy and unbalanced pattern of behavior started when I was a teenager. I was a yearbook editor, captain of the basketball and football cheerleading squads, a member of Beta Club and FCA, and I helped with the school newspaper, participated in extracurricular activities, and worked part time. I'm exhausted just from typing all that! Afraid of letting others down or being without a role to play, I couldn't say no. It's no wonder I almost had a nervous breakdown.

Remember how I shared in chapter 2 that I finally came to a point where I admitted to God and myself that I wasn't fine? It was just a few months before this walk around my college campus. During the first semester of my senior year in college, I hit a breaking point. I remember sitting on the floor in my apartment, sobbing on the phone to my mom. I blurted out questions like, "Will you still love me even if I never accomplish another thing? Even if I don't get a job offer or make the dean's list? What if I don't finish school?" She assured me that she would always love me and begged me to come home.

Four hours later, I walked in the door, sat down, and wept. I didn't know where all of my questions were coming from; I just needed to be able to ask them. I needed to be held so that I could feel safe falling apart.

I returned to classes the next week feeling better, but two weeks later I hit rock bottom again. The darkness was suffocating. I couldn't run from it, I couldn't numb it with alcohol, and I couldn't escape it with busyness. I wanted to end it. One night I went to a party and drank too much alcohol. Driving home that night, I felt hopeless. I didn't want to live anymore because I couldn't fix anything or even figure out why I was so miserable. I doubted I would ever find anything or anyone who could fill me or fulfill me, and I was tired of searching.

I remember seeing a telephone pole and thinking I could just wrap my car around it and everybody would think it was an accident. Scared by my thoughts, I pulled my car over on the side of the road and sat there sobbing. I remember saying, "God, if You're real, I need You to take over. I can't do this anymore." I looked at my hands gripping the steering wheel and imagined His hands there instead. Peace washed over my heart, and I wiped the tears from my eyes and pulled back onto the highway.

I didn't tell anyone what had happened but the next week I saw some flyers on campus advertising a retreat that was being hosted by a nearby church I had visited. Something in my heart moved me to sign up to go.

I believe this was God's way of responding to my cry for help. I was looking for a way out of the darkness, searching for something to fill my emptiness, and God was leading my heart to Him. A few weeks later I went to the retreat and heard messages about His love and His desire for a relationship with me. I had heard some of these things before, but this time the pastor asked a question that made me think he was talking directly to me.

He said, "Have you come to a place where you realize your ways aren't working and you are finally willing to admit that you can't do it anymore? Are you ready to surrender your heart to Jesus?" I was shocked and convinced this man had a direct line to God, because I had said almost those exact words to Him in my car just a few weeks before. That night I surrendered my heart to Christ. It was January of 1989.

Is God's Love Enough?

In the months and years leading up to that night in church, I had heard about God's love many times. I had knowledge in my head about His love, but I didn't realize the power of His unconditional love to fill me and fulfill me. I didn't know how desperately I needed the knowledge of His unfailing love to move from my head to my heart.

I think it finally began to sink in that day as I walked around campus. God showed me all I had been looking for, and how it was Him all along. I had found the answer to my heart's question.

Honestly, though, I wondered how God's love could be enough. I wanted it to be true but I doubted He could fill all the empty places in my heart. Our friend Sam questioned Jesus when He offered her living water that could satisfy her so much she'd never thirst again: "You have nothing to draw with and the well is deep. Where can you get this living water?" (John 4:11). Like Sam, I knew my needs were endless. The well of my heart was deep. I wondered how He could even come close to filling it.

What Sam didn't know was that Jesus wanted to satisfy a deeper thirst in her heart that He had created in her. All He needed to draw with was His Spirit, for it would draw her near to Him. And as far as the depth of the well, it was her heart He was looking into, and she was the only one who could stop Him from reaching the parts that needed Him most.

Jesus helped Sam see that no person or position, such as being someone's wife, could fill the empty places in her heart. Just like He has done with me, and just like He wants to do with you, He showed Sam *what* she was looking for and *where* she could find it. Sam was looking for love that wouldn't fail, even when she did, and that day she found it in Christ.

Proverbs 19:22 says, "What a [woman] desires is unfailing love." The word "desire" comes from the Hebrew word *ta'avah*, which means to greatly long for, deeply desire, or crave. Did you know that unfailing love is mentioned thirty-two times in the Bible, and not once is it attributed to a person? It is only attributed to God.

You see, God put a longing for unfailing love in our hearts because He knew it would lead us back to Him. Only God's unfailing love will fill and fulfill the desires of our hearts. It is the deepest thirst of our souls. Until God's love is enough, nothing else will be.

We see this deep thirst even in King David, who had everything. He had the highest position, unlimited possessions, and great power, yet none of it was enough. He described himself as parched and thirsty for God:

> You God, are my God,
>> earnestly I seek you;
> I thirst for you,
>> my whole being longs for you,
> in a dry and parched land
>> where there is no water. (Ps. 63:1)

Then David went on to describe what he experienced when he drank deeply of God's love:

> I have seen you in the sanctuary
>> and beheld your power and your glory.
> Because your love is better than life,
>> my lips will glorify you.
> I will praise you as long as I live
>> and in your name I will lift up my hands. (vv. 2–4)

Worshiping in Spirit and in Truth

How do we get to a place where God's love can be our "enough"? Let's pick up where we left off with Sam's story. When Jesus told Sam to go and get her husband, she changed the subject by asking Him where she should worship. We already talked about how she might have been distancing herself, diverting His attention, or hiding behind religion.

Then again, maybe she'd felt that aching emptiness we all know when something or someone fails us—the emptiness that cannot be filled by food, family, shopping, friends, sex, alcohol, television, romance novels, or anything else. How many times have we gone to church and hoped we'd have an emotional experience that would fill or fix us? Maybe Sam thought if she went to the right place to worship she'd find that feeling she was looking for.

Let's see what Jesus said when Sam asked Him where she should worship:

> "Woman," Jesus replied, "believe me, a time is coming when you will worship the Father neither on this mountain nor in Jerusalem. You Samaritans worship what you do not know; we worship what we do know, for salvation is from the Jews. Yet a time is coming and has now come when the true worshipers will worship the Father in the Spirit and in truth, for they are the kind of worshipers the Father seeks. God is spirit, and his worshipers must worship in the Spirit and in truth."
>
> The woman said, "I know that Messiah" (called Christ) "is coming. When he comes, he will explain everything to us."
>
> Then Jesus declared, "I, the one speaking to you—I am he." (John 4:21–26)

Jesus helped Sam see that it didn't matter where she worshiped, but *who* and *what* she worshiped. The word *worship* means to feel "an adoring reverence or regard" for a person or thing.[1] Jesus explained that God was looking for worshipers who would worship Him in Spirit and in truth, and then He made a way for Sam to do just that.

Jesus invited her to worship Him in Spirit by offering to pour the living water of His Spirit into the well of her heart, filling the empty places in her soul. He also led her to worship Him in truth by having her acknowledge that she had put others in a place of preeminence where only He belonged. That is why He asked her to go get her husband. When she said she didn't have one, notice how He simply told her, "What you have just said is quite true" (John 4:16–18).

I believe Jesus wanted to help her see the truth: she had been worshiping something physical and something false. Perhaps she had been looking to her husbands, and now the man she was living with, to fill her and fulfill her, believing that her value was determined by their acceptance and approval.

By being honest about her life and the lies she believed, she could start turning toward the truth. She could bring the thirst of her heart to Him. Only then would she find confidence in the power of His love and start living in the security of His promises.

Jesus wants to help us get honest with God and ourselves about what and who we are worshiping. The origin of the word *worship* comes from blending two words to form "worth-ship." When we worship something or someone, we give them great worth in our lives and oftentimes we find our worth in them. We also set our focus on them and eventually they become the very thing we look toward to fill us.

For instance, if we focus on our job (or our marriage) all the time, thinking about how we are doing at work (or home) and what our boss (or husband) thinks about us, we start to find our worth in our performance, and our job (or marriage) can become something we worship. If we are doing well, we feel fulfilled. If we are not doing well, we feel empty and like we have less worth.

Filling the Empty Places in Our Hearts

Our hearts leak and will always end up empty when we find our worth in anything but who we are in Christ. Our value is not measured by what others think of us—but we surely live like it is, don't we? It's almost as though we wake up every morning with an empty jar, like Sam, and walk around holding it out to people or things, hoping they will fill us. We look to our relationships, our stuff, and our status to define us.

From the time we are kids, we look to people: parents, friends, teachers, bosses, boyfriends, ministry leaders, or whoever else is in a position of importance to us. We long for their approval because it gives us a sense of significance, but then we feel like we are only as valuable as our last accomplishment.

As we get older, we look for a man who will bestow on us a sense of beauty and belonging, a sense of being chosen and wanted. We put him in a place of preeminence, hoping he will finally be the one who can satisfy the thirst of our heart for lasting love.

When people don't work, we look to the many possessions the world tells us we need, like newer cars, bigger houses, and trendy clothes. We finally get a newer car and we're so happy. A few months later someone dings it in the parking lot, a kid spills apple juice on the seat, and cracker crumbs are now smashed into the carpet right next to the coffee stain we've been meaning to clean for weeks.

So we head to the mall to get a new outfit, and it feels so good. Then we walk into a meeting and somebody else is wearing it too. All of a sudden the outfit is old and doesn't make us feel so special anymore. Maybe if we could just get a new house—a bigger house—or just some new furniture, then we'd feel better, right?

But that's not all; we vie for positions and put our hope in recognition. We long to be acknowledged. We want to be noticed. Whether it's a calling in ministry or a corner office at work, a plaque on our wall, a title on our door, a promotion, or even an education, we work hard to get to higher places—and then wonder why they are never enough.

Our schedules are full, our minds are full, our stomachs are full, our refrigerators are full, our closets are full, our lives are full. Yet we find ourselves with so many empty places.

Why? Because the wells of our hearts were created to be filled by God alone. The deepest thirst of our soul can only be quenched by Him. Although the people and things I've listed are gifts, so many times we look to the gifts instead of the Giver to fill us and fulfill us with lasting security and significance.

So what do we do when our hearts start tossing and turning with emptiness and uncertainty? We need to stop and ask Jesus to help us see the worth we are placing in other things and the worth we are seeking in other people. One thing that has helped me is to write when-then statements.

For example:

> *When* I start to measure my value by how well I am doing as a _____ (mom, wife, woman, friend, etc.), *then* I will thank God for the gift of my roles and for the gift of His unconditional love that determines my worth.
>
> *When* I feel insecure about my position at work, church, or somewhere else, *then* I will thank God for the high or low position I have on earth and for my position in Christ that secures my significance forever.
>
> *When* I feel an aching emptiness that I'm tempted to fill with food, television, or anything other than God, *then* I will thank God for being the strength of my heart and my portion forever—and remember that He is the One who satisfies the hunger and thirst of my soul.

By recognizing and replacing our emptiness with the fullness of God's promises, we drink the gift of living water. We acknowledge our need, which allows Him to pour His truth into the well of our hearts. I've included thirty-one promises in chapter 12 to encourage you and help you write your own *when-then* statements.

Friend, we don't do any of this because God needs us to. We do this because our hearts were made to worship and find our worth in Him alone. Worship helps us recognize God for who He is as we ascribe great worth to Him. By changing our focus to the Giver, we can then begin to look to Him for our identity and purpose. By worshiping Him for who He is, we remember how valuable we are *in Him* and *to Him*.

Saved and Satisfied

Jesus came to give us more than salvation. He wants us to experience complete satisfaction in Him. As King David shows us, we can only find lasting satisfaction when we continually drink from the source of God's unconditional love, asking God like he did, "Satisfy us in the morning with your unfailing love, that we may sing for joy and be glad all our days" (Ps. 90:14).

I have had so many women tell me, "I know I'm saved, but I'm not satisfied." They know Jesus promised abundant life, but there is nothing abundant in their lives except busyness, obligations, and exhaustion. It's so easy to fall back into the patterns of this world's thinking and the patterns of our old way of living. We let those patterns drive our lives instead of looking for direction and seeking satisfaction in Christ.

It can happen over a period of months, but sometimes it can happen over a period of minutes. We lose sight of Jesus as our confidence and completion, and we start looking to other people and things to fill us. Salvation is a one-time decision, but finding satisfaction in Christ and living in the security of His promises is a daily process.

Jesus wants us to invite Him to look into the well of our hearts each day and show us what, who, and where we are looking to be filled and fulfilled. As we allow Jesus to fill and fulfill us instead, the Holy Spirit quenches our spiritual thirst. We find our soul satisfaction in Him and begin to live with a sense of contentment and confidence based on the unchanging promise of who we are and what we have in Christ.

We become secure as we know and rely on His love more and more. It is a moment by moment, day by day experience where we process our thoughts, emotions, and decisions with God, positioning our hearts to let His perspective redefine ours.

In chapter 4 we are going to see what happens when we live a life completely surrendered to Christ. We will finish our journey with Sam by discovering how Jesus gave her hope for her future despite the pain of her past. She drank deeply of His love that day. Even though she had failed, His love did not fail her. Through His actions and with His words, Jesus told her she was chosen, valuable, loved, forgiven, and free.

The same is true for you and me. We were made for love that isn't measured by our last accomplishment but marked by God's measureless grace. A confident heart is found in a woman who knows beyond the shadow of a doubt that she is loved no matter what. Lasting security comes when we bring the empty well of our hearts to Jesus and ask Him to fill and fulfill us with the security of His unfailing love.

Praying God's Promises

Lord, I pray that You would guide me in Your truth and teach me, for You are God my Savior. I want to learn how to put my hope in You all day, every day. Please help me stop searching for fulfillment in anything or anyone but You. My soul thirsts for You; my body longs for You in this dry and weary land where there is no water. Satisfy me each morning with Your unfailing love so I can sing for joy all the days of my life. I want to be rooted and established in Your love.

I want to have power, together with all the saints, to grasp how wide and long and high and deep the love of Christ is. I want to know this love that surpasses knowledge that I may be filled to the measure of the fullness of God. Thank You that Your love never fails, even when I do. Because Your love is better than life, my lips will glorify You and praise You as long as I live. In Your name I will lift up my hands, Amen.

See Psalms 25:5; 90:14; 63:1; Ephesians 3:17–19; Psalm 63:2–4.

Reflection and Discussion Questions

1. What is the craziest thing you have ever done for love?
2. Think about your desire to find a relationship, a job, a calling, or something else that would satisfy the longings of your heart. Like Sam and me, have you ever looked to something or someone to fill or fulfill you? Describe how that might have shaped the pattern of your thoughts, decisions, and pursuits.
3. Are your closet, your schedule, your mind, and your life full? How about your heart? Are there empty places that you need and want to trust God to fill? If so, list them.
4. "The origin of the word *worship* comes from blending two words to form 'worth-ship.' When we worship something or someone, we give them great worth in our lives and oftentimes we find our worth in them" (p. 58). Where are you most tempted to find your worth? In what area is it hardest to let God define you—and not the world's standards (i.e., career, financial success, motherhood, marriage, or ministry)?

5. Read Proverbs 19:22; Psalm 63:2–4; and Psalm 90:14. What do these verses tell you about God's unfailing love? Have you ever wondered how God's love could be enough?

6. What is the difference between salvation and satisfaction in Christ?

7. "We were made for love that isn't measured by our last accomplishment but marked by God's measureless grace" (p. 62). Write a few when-then statements for areas of your life where you can apply this truth.

For example: *When* I am tempted to measure my value by how well I am doing as a _____ (mom, wife, woman, friend, etc.), I will stop. *Then* I will thank God for His measureless grace that fills my gaps and determines my value, which is not measured by my accomplishments but by His love for me.

4

God Promises Hope for My Future Despite the Pain of My Past

Faith looks back and draws courage; hope looks ahead and keeps desire alive.

John Eldredge and Brent Curtis[1]

God works all things together for good.

You were created for a purpose.

God has a plan for your life.

What do these promises evoke in your heart? Do you believe they are true, or do you sometimes doubt them? I've doubted and I've believed. It's easy to believe God's promises when you haven't had much pain in your life. Yet few of us have walked this far without experiencing bumps and bruises along the way. Many of us have been completely knocked off our feet and wondered if we would ever have the strength to get back up again.

Yet getting back up is often where we find our strength. I remember a friend telling me God wanted to heal the pain of my past and use what I'd experienced to pave the way to His plans for my future. Honestly, I didn't want God to use my pain or my past for anything. I doubted any of it could make me better or stronger, or do any good for anyone, especially me.

I hadn't been a Christian for long, but it felt like the "honeymoon stage" was ending. I was struggling with some painful things in my past that made me doubt God's love and plans. I couldn't figure it out: if God loved me so much, why did He allow these things to happen? If He loved me, why did He let me grow up with so much sadness?

Why would God allow my family to be broken by the long-lasting effects of divorce, shattered by confusion and chaos, shaken by alcohol and drug addictions, and so much more? And why didn't He stop me from the pain I brought on myself, or rescue me from the darkness of depression? The weight of it was too much for my heart to carry. I wondered, *If God's love doesn't fail, then why do I feel like He's failed me?*

Have you ever asked: "If God loves me, why . . . ?" These are the kind of questions that linger in our hearts when we have been wounded or disappointed. When our questions make us doubt God's heart, our pain can lead to bitterness and bondage. Yet in the security of our relationship with Christ, God wants us to ask hard questions and look for answers that usher us into the depths of His redeeming love. He wants us to live in the promise that He offers hope for our future despite the pain of our past. He knows our past and our pain can actually lead us to His plans and hope for our future.

One day I was talking with my friend Wanda while we sat on the beach. She was a safe place to be real, so I unloaded all of my hurts, disappointments, and doubts about God on her. She didn't give me a pat answer. She simply looked at me with understanding in her eyes and told me she was sorry. Then she shared her story with me, which included many disappointments and heartbreaks. I didn't sense doubt or pain in her words. Instead I sensed confidence and hope. She referred to God as "the God of all comfort, who comforts us in all our troubles, so that we can comfort those in any trouble with the comfort we ourselves receive from God" (2 Cor. 1:3–4).

Wanda told me God wanted to heal my hurts and that eventually He could use my pain to comfort others with the same hope He wanted to give me. I could tell she was talking from experience. God's redeeming love was the source of her joy. She had allowed Him to take her pain and give her purpose.

Turning the pages of her Bible to Jeremiah 29, Wanda told me about a promise God had given her to claim: "'For I know the plans I have for you,' declares the LORD, 'plans to prosper you and not to harm you, plans to give you hope and a future'" (Jer. 29:11). I perked up as I heard for the first time that God knows the plans He has for me, and they were plans to give me a future filled with hope, not hurt.

I hoped this meant I could bury the sadness, regrets, and disappointments from my past and count on a happier future. I relished the words of this promise and imagined in my mind what God's plans might look like in my life. Wanda encouraged me to read my Bible and ask God to give me a verse to claim as a promise for my life, one that jumped off the page into my heart when I read it. She then left me on the beach by myself to do just that.

The book of Isaiah was my favorite book in the Bible at the time, I think because God said a lot of what I needed to hear through Isaiah, things like "fear not," "I am with you," and "I love you." I had only read through Isaiah 43 until that day. This time I started there and kept reading until I got to chapter 61.[2] I read slowly as I identified with several of the words in the first verse:

> The Spirit of the Sovereign LORD is on me,
>   because the LORD has anointed me
>   to preach good news to the poor.
> He has sent me to bind up the brokenhearted,
>   to proclaim freedom for the captives
>   and release from darkness for the prisoners. (Isa. 61:1)

Brokenhearted. Captive. Prisoner. Darkness. These words described how I felt for so long. I had been brokenhearted. I had been held captive by fear. I had lived as a prisoner in the darkness of depression. These words were so personal that I wondered if God had written them just for me. I continued to take it all in:

> . . . to proclaim the year of the LORD's favor
>   and the day of vengeance of our God,
> to comfort all who mourn. (v. 2)

I loved the idea of having God's favor, and the "day of vengeance" made me smile too. I assumed it meant God would get back at anyone who had intentionally hurt me. I guess you can say I still had forgiveness issues. Then I read, "comfort all who mourn," and sighed deeply. I had been mourning the loss of so many things, especially dreams of a happily-ever-after that hadn't come true. I kept reading:

> . . . and provide for those who grieve in Zion—
> to bestow on them a crown of beauty instead of
> ashes,
> the oil of gladness
> instead of mourning,
> and a garment of praise
> instead of a spirit of despair.
> They will be called oaks of righteousness,
> a planting of the LORD
> for the display of his splendor. (v. 3)

I imagined wearing a "garment of praise instead of a spirit of despair." The thought of being called an oak of righteousness made me feel strong inside. I had always felt more like a pine tree that had been tossed by the winds of my emotions, defined by my circumstances, and uprooted by life's storms. An oak represented strength and courage, just what I longed for.

My heart filled with hope, so I went back and read the verses again. I guess I had only skimmed the opening sentence earlier, because when I read it a second time, I felt confused. The part about preaching good news to the poor was especially concerning. I automatically inserted question marks. *The Spirit of the Lord is on me? Because the Lord has anointed me? To preach good news to the poor?*

Running from My Pain

It didn't make any sense. Then I recalled Wanda telling me God wanted to heal the pain of my past and comfort the brokenness in my heart so I could share His hope with others.

I squeezed my eyes shut and started praying, asking God to show me why He led me to those verses. I sat there waiting, and the weirdest thing I had ever experienced happened: I saw an image on the screen of my mind, like a video. In this mental movie I could see myself sharing my story with other women, and it scared me half to death.

I opened my eyes and slammed my Bible shut. Then I started making a deal with God. I said something like, "Lord, I will do anything for You. I will lead Bible studies. I will tithe over 10 percent. I will share the gospel with strangers. I will move to Africa. I'm willing to eat beans and rice for a long time, but please, please, please don't make me share my story."

The thought of sharing my story made me sick to my stomach. You see, for over twenty years I had lived behind a mask. I was good at pretending everything was okay, and I liked it that way. I didn't want anyone to know about the pain of my past. I didn't want to talk about it or deal with it. I was still ashamed of it and wanted it to go away.

There were obviously things I needed to deal with, but I was afraid I would fall apart or slip back into a depression if I talked with God or others about my brokenness. I thought people would feel sorry for me or look down on me. I wanted God to write a new story, one I could be proud to tell others about.

Instead of studying Isaiah 61:1–3 and asking God to heal my broken heart, set me free from the captivity of my fear, and help me understand what had led me into the darkness of my depression, I ignored those verses. I wanted to leave my past in my past, so I decided to focus instead on the promise I liked a whole lot better in Jeremiah 29:11.

For the next ten years I went about my business, looking for the plans God had to prosper me and not to harm me, to give me a future and a hope. I served Him with all my heart and soul, doing my best to give Him some good-Christian-girl story material. I joined a church, taught Bible studies, led door-to-door evangelism outreaches on university campuses, and volunteered at my church. I even raised support to be a part-time staff person with a campus-based Christian ministry while working full-time in a secular career.

All the while I was running. Running from my past and my pain. Eventually, I would discover that I was also running from the healing work God wanted to do in my heart.

Running toward God's Plans

Unlike me, instead of running away, the Samaritan woman ran back to the people she'd been running from:

> Then, leaving her water jar, [Sam] went back to the town and said to the people, "Come, see a man who told me everything I ever did. Could this be the Messiah?" They came out of the town and made their way toward him. (John 4:28–30)

Sam had walked to the well alone that day carrying the weight of her pain and a jar to fill with water. After meeting Jesus, she left behind the jar she carried as well as the shame she wore, and with it all of the rejection and regrets that were tied to her past. She ran back to the people she had been running from. How could she be so different, so confident, so free? Something had changed.

For the first time, Sam realized that her Messiah knew her: all she had done and all that had been done to her. He knew her failures and her shame, and He loved her completely. He had chosen to come to her, of all people. When He spoke truth into the most wounded places in her heart, He poured out His healing power. And she received it. His love seeped into her pain and released Sam from her past. She knew then that she didn't have to hide or run from it anymore.

Hurts That Rob Us of Hope

Is there pain from your yesterdays or disappointments in your today that have caused you to lose your confidence and hope? When you have been wounded, the risk of getting hurt again seems more costly, and perhaps even more likely, doesn't it? The things that hurt us are as varied as the lies we believe because of them:

- Like my friend who was sexually abused by a neighbor when she was eight years old. Shame convinced her she would always be dirty and worthless.
- Like my friend who was raped at knifepoint by a masked stranger the week of her college graduation. Fear held her for years in a personal prison, telling her she'd never be free.
- Like my family of origin that was devastated by the destruction of addiction. Codependency told us things would only get better if we tried harder.
- Like my friend who was married and divorced multiple times. Condemnation convinced her she'd never be good enough for a man or God.
- Like a woman I know whose mother called her names and criticized everything she did. Humiliation holds her hostage, convincing her she'll always be useless.
- Like my friend who had an abortion when she was a teenager. Paralyzing grief and disgrace convinced her that God could never use her in ministry.
- Like me, who gave away my virginity at sixteen although I had vowed to wait until I was married. Sorrow

convinced me I had lost a part of my soul I could never get back.

- Like my friend whose son is in prison awaiting trial as a sex offender. False blame keeps her up at night and constantly tells her she must have done something wrong as a mother.
- Like a woman I met recently who refused a drug test at work and lost her job. Alcoholism convinced her to live in secret. She feels like her life is ruined now.
- Like you . . .

I wonder where you have been and what you have been through. Are there things you have done or things that have been done to you that have left you feeling hopeless? The pain of our past makes it hard to believe God's promise of hope for our future. It's easy to lose confidence in Him and in ourselves. My prayer for you right now is that God would open the eyes of your heart so that "you may know the hope to which he has called you . . . and his incomparably great power for us who believe" (Eph. 1:18–19).

Hope Is on the Way

Hope comes when we allow Jesus to search our hearts and bring truth into our wounded places, like Sam did. He wants us to "trust in Him, so that [we will] overflow with hope by the power of the Holy Spirit" (Rom. 15:13). When we let Jesus pour His healing power into our lives, His love flows into our pain and cleanses the wounds from our past. As we come to know God and fully rely on His love for us, we stop allowing the past to determine our future.

It took me awhile to get to that place. My husband and I had been married for several years when we started experiencing severe tension. I got angry easily but didn't know why. Knowing we needed help, we attended a conference where Gary Smalley talked about unresolved anger that we sometimes bring into marriage. I realized that night my anger as an adult stemmed from my years of disappointment as a child because I never got the happily-ever-after I wanted. My hope had been deferred and my heart had become sick.

When I was in elementary school, I used to make bouquets out of azaleas and walk down the aisle of my dad's long driveway lined with magnolia trees, imagining a prince waiting for me on the porch. Those were little girl dreams I thought I had left behind, but God showed me that in some ways I was still demanding they come true. My broken dreams had become bitter expectations; I wanted my husband to make up for all that my dad had never been as a father to me or as a husband to my mom.

I was bound and determined to secure my future by creating my own version of a happily-ever-after. When it didn't turn out so happy, I was angry and afraid. My unrealistic expectations erupted in the form of critical words toward my husband, telling him how to be the husband and dad I wanted him to be. I thought if JJ could be those things, my broken dreams could be put back together. My husband would provide security and shelter for the little-girl-heart that was still crushed inside my adult body. Then I would have hope for my future and become the confident woman and wife I wanted to be.

God showed me I needed to forgive my father and release my feelings of bitterness, abandonment, disappointment, and hurt. I also needed to confess the sin of my unrealistic expectations and let go of what I thought was my right to a "happily-ever-after." God also showed me I needed to find my security and hope in Him alone by letting Him be the

Father I longed for. I needed to grieve some of the things I wanted that I would never have. I also needed to invite God into those hurting places so He could bind up my broken heart and set me free from captivity to my fear that I would never have a happy ending.

Letting God Write Our Stories

As I released my grip, God began to heal my heart and my marriage. The work He did in my marriage was the beginning of a bigger work He was doing in my life. Over a period of eighteen months He walked me through a season of looking back so I could move forward. God used that time to "rebuild [my] ancient ruins and restore the [broken] places [in my heart that had been] long devastated" (Isa. 61:4).

During that period of time, I attended a women's retreat where a speaker shared her story of totally surrendering to God's call, and how it led to healing and hope in her life. As God would have it, she taught on the verses I had vowed to ignore: Isaiah 61:1–3. I tried to silence the memories her message evoked, but I couldn't.

I thought of the day, ten years earlier, when I sat on the beach and read them for the first time. I cried as I realized God had been waiting all this time for me to come to Him for hope and healing. That night I surrendered everything , and told God I would be willing to share the pain of my past if it meant others could find healing and hope through my story.

Later, while I was getting ready to go to sleep, I sensed God nudging me to tell my roommate what had happened. Lisa was a friend from Bible study but not someone I knew very well. I wasn't sure what she would think, but I told her my story, specifically about my struggle with depression and how I'd come to know Christ.

She listened with tears in her eyes. Then Lisa told me she had also battled depression in high school but never told anyone because she was so ashamed. We sat on the edge of our beds and prayed that God would give us both the courage to share a chapter of our lives we had hidden as a shameful secret, even if it meant setting just one more captive free.

We can trust God's plans as we realize that His story is being written in ours. His power is perfected in the broken places we consider to be our greatest weaknesses—our most vulnerable emotions we don't want anyone to know about. In those hiding places, God calls us out of captivity. When we're willing to let Him, He brings hope for our future despite the pain of our past.

It took me the longest time to understand and believe God could use my mistakes and hurts for His greatest purposes if I would allow Him to change me through them. I wanted God to burn the pages of my old story and write what I thought would be a better story for Him to tell. Instead He wanted to finish what He started, completing the work He had begun in me with a narrative that would bind up my broken heart and set this captive free. What story is God wanting to write in your life? Will you let Him?

The Freedom of Forgiveness

During my season of looking back so I could move forward, God showed me several areas of my life that needed restoration. I decided to write out a timeline of my life and asked the Holy Spirit, whom Jesus referred to as our Counselor, to help me see the wounds I had buried in my past.

With each wound, I asked Jesus to heal the pain and claimed Isaiah 51:3, "The LORD will surely comfort [you] and will look with compassion on all [your] ruins; he will make [your]

deserts like Eden, [your] wastelands like the garden of the
LORD."

Over time I started to release the pain of my regrets, shame,
fear, and disappointments. Although I knew God wanted me
to deal with my past, I also knew God did not want me to
dwell in the past. He would whisper to my heart again and
again, *See, Renee, I am doing a new thing! Now it springs up;
do you see it? I am making a way in the desert and streams
in the wasteland* (Isa. 43:18–19).

A painful crossroad in my journey came when I had to decide whether I would attend my college class reunion. While
I was in the pit of depression during college, I had been
deeply hurt by an old friend who would be at the reunion. I
had never forgiven her, and I was afraid that if I saw her my
wounded emotions would surface.

Although I wanted to stay home, I sensed God wanted
me to go. I felt like He wanted me to revisit those physical
and emotional places where I always believed I had walked
alone. The Holy Spirit showed me I needed to remake my
memories by seeing how Jesus had been there all along, and
then replace the lies my wounds had led me to believe with
new truths He was teaching me through Scripture.

One day while I was wrestling over this decision, a very
hard yet powerful revelation came. God showed me sin I didn't
want to see. The conflict with my old friend had led to bitterness in my heart, and the Holy Spirit helped me see that
I had played a role in it. I needed to forgive her and ask her
to forgive whatever I had done to upset her so much. Ouch!
It was hard to accept, but I wanted freedom no matter what
it would cost me.

I surrendered to what God was showing me and decided
to go to the reunion, but I was still afraid. To prepare myself,
I spent time praying and reading my Bible, asking God to

remind me of His perspective and fill my insecurities with His assurance. I wanted to walk into the reunion as a "new creation," not the broken person I had been ten years before.

During my three hour drive back to Meredith College, I listened to worship music and some great Bible teaching. By the time I arrived, I was so filled up with God's perspective and promises, I literally wanted to find my old friend and pursue restoration in our relationship. I was not the same person I had been when I received the invitation. Confidence came as I followed God's command to seek and offer forgiveness.

Forgiving those who have hurt us is hard. Often we are afraid to forgive because it might open us up to be hurt again. We hesitate to ask others for forgiveness because they might think we're the only one who did something wrong—and they won't think they need to change. Or we're afraid if we bring something up again we're going to unearth bitterness we don't want to deal with, so we just leave it buried. But any time we bury a hurt that's still alive, it just rises from the dead to haunt us.

In Ephesians 4, the Bible tells us to "Be completely humble and gentle; be patient, bearing with one another in love... forgiving each other, just as in Christ God forgave you" (vv. 2, 32). Forgiveness was demonstrated on a cross where Jesus displayed His perfect love by dying for imperfect people. At Calvary, Jesus laid down His pain and hurt and chose love and forgiveness instead. His forgiveness frees us to forgive ourselves and others.

Of course, some things are much harder and take more time to forgive than others. When I am really having a hard time forgiving or finding healing from a deep wound, I ask Jesus to cover my wounds with His blood. As Scripture tells us:

> In him we have redemption through his blood, the forgiveness of sins, in accordance with the riches of God's grace

that he lavished on us. With all wisdom and understanding
. . . he was pierced for our transgressions, he was crushed for
our iniquities; the punishment that brought us peace was on
him, and by his wounds we are healed. (Eph. 1:7–8; Isa. 53:5)

You can't go back and change the circumstances or relationships that have wounded you, but you can go back
and process the pain with Jesus. In fact, you won't move
forward with God until you do. And left unresolved, the
pain from yesterday can keep you from having confident
hope for tomorrow.

Ask God to show you the broken places in your past you
have carried into your future. Make a timeline of your life
with key events, and write down any painful emotions and
memories. Then ask the Holy Spirit to remind you where
you have been, what those events caused, how far from God
those things took you, and how they hurt you and others.

Invite God to enter into those memories with you. Give
yourself time to grieve your losses as you ask Jesus to heal them
with the power of His Holy Spirit as you focus your thoughts
on transforming truths in His Word. As He shows you broken
places, ask Him to bind up every wound with His healing
touch and set you free from any captivity that has held you
until now. Pray His promises. Cry if you need to. Just please
take time, sweet friend, to heal so you can find hope again.

From Broken to Beautiful

Hope for your future will come when you allow Jesus to
enter into the broken places of your life and do something
beautiful. He wants to heal your heart and your hurts, just
like He did with our friend Sam. Did you notice that Sam

didn't wait for a new story? She allowed Jesus to take her mess and make it His message. She was willing to become His messenger.

> Many of the Samaritans from that town believed in him because of the woman's testimony, "He told me everything I ever did." So when the Samaritans came to him, they urged him to stay with them, and he stayed two days. And because of his words many more became believers.
>
> They said to the woman, "We no longer believe just because of what you said; now we have heard for ourselves, and we know that this man really is the Savior of the world." (John 4:39–42)

Sam had been loved, so she could love. She had been forgiven, so she could forgive. She had been set free, so she could lead other captives to freedom. She knew she belonged to Him and invited others into the Father's love.

She had been broken but now she was beautiful—an offering of God's forgiveness and grace. And the people from her small town wanted what she had, so they followed her to Jesus. Most of us won't experience full restoration and hope that quickly, but Sam's story does give us a picture of what God wants to do in our lives.

God Has a Plan for Your Life

If you are living and breathing, God has a purpose for you. Your destiny has not been fulfilled. No matter what you have done or what has been done to you, God has a plan for your life! He wants to use everything He has brought you to, to bring you *through*. Not a single thing in your life will be wasted. God will use your past and present to prepare you for your future.

So, how do you discover the plans God has for you? We're going to talk in depth about it in chapter 8, but first let's go back and read the *premise* that follows the promise we read in Jeremiah 29. After God declares He knows the plans He has for us, plans to prosper us and give us a future filled with hope, He says, "Then you will call on me and come and pray to me, and I will listen to you. You will seek me and find me when you seek me with all your heart" (Jer. 29:12–13).

God's plans for us are found when we surrender ours and seek His each day. God's plans unfold each time we come to Him, talk to Him, and really believe He's listening.

Learning to live in the security of God's promises is a daily journey of dependence. As we process the pain of our yesterdays, learn through the disappointments of our todays, and face some fears in our tomorrows, doubts will still creep up and threaten to steal our hope. But each time that happens, we can stop and seek God's perspective in that place.

We can ask Him to show us His purpose by revealing what is true about who we are and what we have been through that caused us to start doubting ourselves. We can ask Him to help us redefine our future—not through the filter of our past and our pain, but through the power of His life-changing promises.

Do you know what happens when we do that moment by moment, day by day, and doubt by doubt? God tells us in Jeremiah 29:14, "I will be found by you . . . and will bring you back from captivity."

We find Him again and again. We find the One who can lead us to freedom from the captivity of our doubts and insecurities. I know this without a doubt because I have walked it, wrestled with it, resisted it, and finally surrendered to it.

God's love is not only perfect and unfailing, it redeems and restores. His truth cuts to the core of our struggles, bringing purpose to our pain, redemption from our past, and hope for our future!

Praying God's Promises

Lord, You know the plans You have for me, plans to prosper me and not to harm me; plans to give me hope and a future. I'm calling upon You and praying to You, and You promise that You will listen to me. You say that I will find You when I seek You with all my heart. Open the eyes of my heart so that I can know the hope to which You have called me and Your incomparably great power for us who believe. Rebuild my ancient ruins and restore places devastated long ago in my heart.

Help me forgive those who have hurt me, just as in Christ You forgave me. Despite the pain of my past, You offer hope for my future and want to do a new thing in my life, making a way in the desert and streams in my wastelands. When my soul is downcast, I will call this to mind and I will have hope. Because of Your great love, I am not consumed, for Your compassions never fail. They are new every morning; great is Your faithfulness! In Jesus' name, Amen.

See Jeremiah 29:11–13; Ephesians 1:18–19; Isaiah 61:4; Ephesians 4:2, 32; Isaiah 43:18–19; Lamentations 3:20–23.

Reflection and Discussion Questions

1. Has the pain of your past ever made it hard for you to believe God's promises and plans for your future? What do you sense He wants to change in your perspective?
2. Can you think of a time when you asked: "If God loves me, then why . . . ?" If so, what happened that led you to ask that question?

3. Read 2 Corinthians 1:3–4. How has God comforted you in your troubles so that you can comfort others with the same hope He has given you?

4. How have past hurts robbed you of hope and affected your relationships today?

5. Read Isaiah 61:1–3. What are some things God promises in these verses that you are asking Him to fulfill in your life?

6. Describe how unforgiveness can hold you hostage and keep you from moving forward in hope. Is there someone you need to forgive or seek forgiveness from?

7. Have you ever run from the story God has written in your life? Do you sense Him inviting you, like Sam, to share the "from broken to beautiful" pieces with someone who needs hope? Will you?

5

Living beyond the Shadow of My Doubts

"Why are you frightened?" [Jesus] asked. "Why are your hearts filled with doubt?"

Luke 24:38 NLT

Remember that day I was getting ready in the bathroom and discovered the shadow of my doubt? I wish I could say that as soon as I discovered it, it went away. But the story doesn't end with me zipping up my suitcase, driving to the airport, and having God zap me with confidence. That day as I turned around and stood facing the mirror in my bathroom, not only did I realize I was no longer standing in the shadow, but I realized I had created the shadow by blocking the light.

Shadows are created all around us when something blocks light. So it is with the shadow of doubt. In the same way, when we focus on our insecurities we cast a shadow of doubt in our minds by blocking the light of God's truth in our hearts.

We were not designed to block the light or to be the light. We were created to live in the light in such a way that our life stories tell about the light and our confidence in Christ draws others to the light. I love how John the Baptist is described as "a witness to testify concerning that light, so that through him all might believe. He himself was not the light; he came only as a witness to the light" (John 1:7–8).

The same is true for you and me. Jesus said, "I am the light of the world. Whoever follows me will never walk in darkness, but will have the light of life" (John 8:12). When we follow Him, we find our confidence in Him and our lives become a message about Him, the One who came to illuminate our darkness with His redeeming love.

On the day that I discovered the shadow of my doubt, I had not been following Jesus—not completely. If I had stayed close to Him in my thoughts, I would have been thinking about what the women at the conference were going to think about Him, not about me. I would have been talking to God about where they were spiritually, and asking how He wanted to encourage them through me.

We find ourselves in the shadow of doubt many times because our thoughts are mostly about ourselves: how we're performing and what others are thinking about us.

Think about it for just a minute. As you went through your day today, how many times did you wonder if you were measuring up to someone's expectations? Maybe you wondered whether your kids felt like you paid enough attention to them, or whether your manager valued your suggestion during the meeting. Or maybe you wondered if anyone liked the dinner you cooked, or even noticed all the trouble you went through to plan and prepare it.

Changing My Focus

It's not that these thoughts are bad. It's just that when we focus our attention on ourselves, we turn our attention away from God. We leave no room in our thoughts to listen to what He is thinking about us, because we have given that place away to be occupied by other people's opinions. We become overly concerned about what others think of us instead of what God thinks about us.

The Bible explains what happens when we become self-focused. Paul says "the mind set on the flesh is death, but the mind set on the Spirit is life and peace" (Rom. 8:6 NASB). You see, God created us for so much more than self-preservation or self-promotion. When we follow our natural inclination to preserve and promote ourselves or perform for others, we eventually end up in a place of darkness and doubt. It's just too much pressure. Even if we achieve success or have a few good days, eventually it won't be enough, because we can't maintain it.

If I wanted to walk out of the shadow of my doubts, I knew I would have to take my eyes off myself and turn them toward the light. As I finished packing my suitcase and getting ready, I asked God to show me how to change my focus.

First, I had to turn my thoughts completely toward Him by thinking about His strengths instead of my weaknesses. I recalled promises in the Bible that reminded me of who He is and how He wants to work in my life. I thought about several of my favorite verses and even read them out loud to myself.

Then I remembered another child of God who became paralyzed by fear and insecurity. His name was Gideon. From reading his story, I knew he had defeated his enemies and his doubts by focusing his thoughts on what God said about him instead of what he thought about himself.

One day God sent an angel to Gideon while he was hiding in a winepress threshing wheat. Normally people would thresh wheat outside, but Gideon was afraid of his enemies, the Midianites. He knew they might see him in the fields, so he went for cover.

> When the angel of the LORD appeared to Gideon, he said, "The LORD is with you, mighty warrior."
>
> "Pardon me, my lord," Gideon replied, "but if the LORD is with us, why has all this happened to us? Where are all his wonders that our ancestors told us about when they said, 'Did not the LORD bring us up out of Egypt?' But now the LORD has abandoned us and given us into the hand of Midian."
>
> The LORD turned to him and said, "Go in the strength you have and save Israel out of Midian's hand. Am I not sending you?"
>
> "Pardon me, my lord," Gideon asked, "but how can I save Israel? My clan is the weakest in Manasseh, and I am the least in my family." (Judg. 6:12–15)

God Is Not Limited by Our Limitations

Just like us, Gideon doubted his strength and abilities. Immediately, his insecurities started shouting excuses, listing all his inadequacies. Do you ever doubt God could use you because of your limitations or weaknesses?

God wasn't limited by Gideon's limitations, and He's not limited by ours either. He didn't want Gideon to depend on his own strength. God wanted Gideon to depend on His strength. God was going to conquer the Midianites, but He invited Gideon to join Him.

Perhaps it was because He knew that, while conquering the Midianites, Gideon would also conquer his personal enemies of doubt and fear. Often God will call you beyond your limitations to do something that requires faith. It's not so much about what He wants you to do as what He wants to do in you, as you depend on Him.

Getting Past Our Past

One thing that triggered Gideon's doubt was his perception of himself based on his past. He said his family was the weakest and he was the least of them all. It's important for us to realize that damaged emotions and insecurities from our past have a powerful influence over how we see ourselves today. Are there negative things from your childhood or family history that have cast a shadow of doubt over your destiny?

As a young girl, I felt like my family was weak and I was the least. When I was growing up, I knew very few people whose parents were divorced. Since mine were, I felt "less than" when I was with friends whose families were whole and happy. Not only did I feel "less than," we had less than most people.

Although my dad had a big fancy house, my brothers and I lived with my mom in a very modest duplex and drove a station wagon that had more dents in it than the moon. We called it "the wreck." I don't know how dirt got in there, or why it stayed in there, but I remember in the back of our station wagon we had little weeds growing. It's funny now, but it was embarrassing as a kid. Making things worse, my dad wouldn't always pay child support, which made me think we must not be worth enough for him to take care of us.

When doubt washes over me, often it is because something has happened to trigger my old emotions and create thoughts in my mind that are similar to those I had as a child. Sometimes that hurt little girl still has too much say in my heart. If I listen to her, powerful yet immature emotions from my past rise to the surface. But they are not truth in my life. The insecurities from your past are not the truth in your life either. As we look at our doubts and develop confident hearts, it's going to be important to recognize negative emotions from our past that keep us from living confidently in our present and future.

We'll also need to realize our family of origin does not define our true identity. Once we become daughters of the King, we have a royal inheritance that determines who we are. Gideon had to stop thinking of himself as the runt of his family and start seeing himself as a child of God, a mighty warrior in his Father's eyes. Whether we had a great family or not, our hearts will only find lasting confidence when we find our identity as children of God.

Other Triggers of Doubt

I love how honest Gideon was about his insecurities. He told the angel of the Lord why he questioned God's presence and doubted His promises. Distrust had crept in through the cracks of his thoughts as Gideon remembered recent conflicts and defeats with the Midianites. As I stood in my bathroom that day with my shadow, I needed to get honest with God, too. I thought back on the events of my week and asked Him to show me what got me so focused on myself and sent me into the darkness of doubt.

Like Gideon, I had fallen into the comparison trap, comparing my abilities to other speakers who had been booked for an upcoming event with me. Self-doubt convinced me I wasn't as gifted as they were. I also had a conflict with a friend that week that made me wonder if I should even be in women's ministry. *After all,* my doubt whispered, *if I couldn't maintain healthy relationships at all times in all areas, how could I help others?*

To top it all off, I received an email with feedback from recent events. There were several positive comments and one criticism. Forgetting about the compliments, I couldn't stop thinking about one person's critical words. In the face of comparison, conflict, and criticism, I took my eyes off God's strength and focused on my weaknesses. I was just like Gideon, only I was hiding in a bathroom instead of a winepress.

Do you ever compare yourself to others you admire and feel like you're not as gifted, smart, well-balanced, capable, or beautiful as they are? When conflict arises at work or at home, do you blame yourself or wonder if there is a flaw in your personality that is causing the dispute? Have someone's critical words ever caused you to doubt you could do certain things?

These are just a few triggers that can lead us into that yucky place of insecurity, a place that makes us want to run and hide from our enemies, whether our enemy is a person, a feeling, or even ourselves.

Although Gideon had been tempted to look back, God challenged him to look ahead. He could see beyond who Gideon was to who he could become. God had promised Gideon he would defeat his enemies, and he would not fight alone. "The LORD answered, 'I will be with you, and you will strike down all the Midianites, leaving none alive'" (Judg. 6:16).

Gideon's first steps out of the shadow of doubt would require he focus on God's promise and power, not himself. Eventually, with God's help, Gideon defeated his enemies and his doubts.

Turning toward the Truth

Before that day in my bathroom with God and my shadow, I thought doubt was simply a negative emotion. I saw doubt as one of my weaknesses, a lapse of faith, a dip in self-confidence. I wanted God to take it away or heal me, but then I realized the shadow of doubt had been cast over my thoughts and emotions because I had stopped living in the security of God's promises. That is how I ended up paralyzed by the darkness.

What about you? How many of these doubts have lured you into the shadows?

I'm not good enough.

I'm such a failure.

I'm always disappointing someone.

God can't use me.

I don't have anything special to offer.

I worry too much.

I can't balance my life.

I can't follow God consistently.

I'll never change.

How often do you agree with these whispers of doubt and find yourself living in discouragement and defeat? Have you felt paralyzed by uncertainty and allowed it to keep you from walking forward with God in faith?

That day in the bathroom, God changed the way I process my doubts. When I find myself standing in the shadow of doubt, I ask Him to show me what triggered my doubt and got me to start turning away from His truth. I ask Him to shine the light of His Word on my heart so I can see His reality versus the lies I am believing.

That day was a turning point. I wanted to burn the image in my mind. Turning away from the shadow—turning toward the light. *Turning* would be crucial.

Turning away from self
Turning toward God
Turning away from doubt
Turning toward truth
Turning away from darkness
Turning toward light

Turning is crucial for us as we learn to live beyond the shadows of our doubts. Turning toward God, so we can listen to what He says about who we are and what we can do. Turning toward truth, so we can know who He is and what He wants to do through our lives as we depend on Him. Turning toward the light of God's promises for us in every area of our lives—as a woman, a mom, a wife, a friend, a leader, a follower of Jesus—so our life can be about living, loving, and leading others to the light of God's truth as we walk it out in our everyday lives.

Instead of waiting for God to zap us with confidence and remove our doubts, let's ask God to use our doubts to draw us into a deeper place of dependence on Him and His promises. It's not necessarily going to be easy, because it requires *turning*, but it is possible and worth what it takes to turn. Turning leads to transforming, as we allow our thoughts to be made new, and transforming leads to believing as God's thoughts become our truth. Are you ready to start turning?

Praying God's Promises

Lord, thank You that in Christ I am a chosen woman, a royal priest, a holy daughter, a woman belonging to God. Thank You that I may declare the praises of Him who called me out of darkness into His wonderful light. Jesus, You are the light

*of the world! You promise that when I follow You, I will not
walk in darkness but will have the light of life. I want to follow You with all my heart and in each of my thoughts. Take
me beyond the shadows of my doubts and teach me how to
rely on the power of Your promises.*

*When doubt overshadows my thoughts, help me shift my
focus back to You, remembering that the mind fixed on the
flesh is death, but the mind fixed on the Spirit is life and peace.
Thank You Lord, my God, that You go with me, to fight for
me against my enemies of insecurity and inadequacy and give
me victory. In all these things, I am more than a conqueror
through Him who loves me. In Jesus' name I pray, Amen.*

See 1 Peter 2:9; John 8:12; 1:7–8; Romans 8:6; Deuteronomy 20:4; Romans
8:37.

Reflection and Discussion Questions

1. "When we focus our attention on ourselves, we turn
   our attention away from God. We leave no room in
   our thoughts to listen to what He is thinking about us,
   because we have given that place away to be occupied
   by other people's opinions" (p. 87). Whose thoughts do
   you tend to focus on the most throughout your day—
   yours, others', or God's?
2. How many times today did you wonder if you were
   measuring up to someone's expectations of you? List
   as many as you can think of.
3. Do you have any limitations or weaknesses that make
   you doubt God can use you—or would want to? If so,
   describe them and why they make you doubt God can
   use you.
4. The angel of the Lord told Gideon, "Go in the strength
   you have . . . am I not sending you? . . . I will be with

you" (Judg. 6:14–16). With that promise in mind, what doubts are you currently facing that you sense God wants you to conquer with Him and depend on His strength to overcome?

5. Review the section in this chapter on "Getting Past Our Past." Write down anything from your past that triggers old emotions that lead to insecurity and self-doubt.

6. What are some other triggers that cause you to doubt yourself (e.g., failure, fear, conflict, discouragement, comparison, worry, criticism, tiredness)?

7. Have you viewed doubt as an emotional weakness in the past? Have you ever asked God to take it away and zap you with confidence? Describe if and how you are beginning to see the struggle with insecurity as part of your spiritual journey.

6

When Doubt Whispers "I'm Not Good Enough"

We've got to get our good enough from Jesus. When we belong to Him, we're clothed in His righteousness, forever beloved and accepted; a constant recipient of His steadfast love and grace.

Gary Morland

Sometimes I'll be thinking about something I want to do or something I sense God calling me to do, and a feeling of doubt suddenly washes over me and whispers to my heart: *You can't do that. You're not good enough.*

Out of the blue, I'll just get that awful, insecure sense of not being good enough. For the longest time I didn't tell anyone about my insecurities, because I figured if I told them all the reasons I thought I wasn't good enough, they'd see my flaws and agree with me. I was convinced I was the only one who struggled with doubt.

However, I didn't always call it doubt. Maybe you don't either. I sometimes called it worry: worry that I was going to disappoint someone, worry that I might make a mistake and get criticized for it, worry that I would get started but not be able to finish. Other times I'd call it fear: fear that I wouldn't measure up, fear that I'd look stupid, fear that I'd look prideful while thinking I could do something special for God, fear that I'd fail, fear that I would be rejected.

What I've realized over the past few years is that although these feelings may end up as fear or worry, their source is self-doubt. I can look back now and see a pattern of thinking that led to my pattern of believing I wasn't good enough.

Chosen or Rejected?

In my search for "happily-ever-after," I started praying for a godly husband. Soon after I became a Christian, I met this really cute churchgoing guy who lived in my apartment community. Not only was he cute, he loved Jesus. He left Bible verses on my door and invited me to Bible studies at his church. I couldn't believe how quickly God brought this kind of man into my life. We'll call him Mike, although that is not his real name.

Mike and I had a storybook Christian romance. We talked about our favorite Bible verses, prayed together, and went no further than holding hands because we wanted to keep our relationship pure. All of our church friends thought we made such a cute couple and would be great partners in life and ministry. A few months after we met, we started talking and praying about marriage. We talked to our pastor, and not too long after, Mike proposed. Our plans were in motion as soon as we chose a wedding date.

Two weeks into our engagement, he called and asked me out for dinner. That night he looked at me from across the table and shocked me with these words: "I've made a horrible mistake. You are not the one God wants me to marry, and I'm so sorry."

I was devastated. I don't even remember what I said. I just remember being dropped off at my apartment, walking inside like a zombie, and weeping with my roommate, who was getting married in a month. I was a bridesmaid and a rejected bride who was about to become homeless. It was horrible. I cried all night long, and on and off for several days. I remember wondering what horrible defect I had that made my fiancé decide I wasn't good enough.

Some mornings my heart hurt so badly I would wake up crying, roll out of bed, and land on my knees. I couldn't face my day without looking into my Father's face. I'd ask Him to give me strength to get through the shame of being rejected. Sometimes I would open my Bible and just smell the pages. I'd also read God's promises and insert my name in them, claiming them as though they were written just for me.

> "Do not be afraid; [Renee] you will not be put to
> shame.
> Do not fear disgrace; you will not be humiliated.
> You will forget the shame of your youth
> and remember no more the reproach of your
> widowhood.
> For your Maker is your husband [Renee]—
> the LORD Almighty is his name—
> the Holy One of Israel is your Redeemer;
> he is called the God of all the earth.
> The LORD will call you back [Renee]
> as if you were a wife deserted and distressed in
> spirit—

a wife who married young,
only to be rejected," says your God. (Isa. 54:4–6)

Over time, I learned through promises like these and others that I was God's beloved and He would never reject me. I wrote verses on index cards and carried them around with me, and eventually I started to believe I was "a crown of splendor in the LORD's hand; a royal diadem in the hand of [my] God" (Isa. 62:3).

As months passed, I could feel God picking up the broken pieces and putting my heart back together. I started going to Christmas parties and company picnics with guys from church and hanging out with new friends from work. After about a year, I was doing really well—and guess who showed up at my door? Yep, it was Mike. He wanted me to prayerfully consider restoring our relationship. I know what you're thinking: *Don't even go there.* Right? Believe me, my friends threatened to picket in front of my apartment holding up signs that said, "Get away from her!"

Second Chances

I knew I loved a God of second chances and that He was a redeeming God. I wondered if He wanted to redeem our story, so I gave Mike a second chance. Now you'd better believe I practically made him sign in blood that he would not dump me again. He promised he had prayed about it and gotten godly counsel.

We started dating again, and a couple months later we talked about marriage. He already had the engagement ring I'd given back to him. I don't remember how long it took, but eventually he proposed again. I accepted and started shopping for dresses. This time it took four weeks. He called. We met for dinner, and he dumped me again!

But I got smart this time; I did not give him back the ring. I held it as collateral to get Mike to go with me to see a counselor. After the first breakup, I was convinced something was wrong with me. This time I was determined to find out what was wrong with him. That way we could be defective together. The counselor decided Mike had a fear of commitment. It made me feel less rejected to have a label for it, although the pain would only get worse before it got any better.

Soon after we started seeing a counselor, I woke up at 3 o'clock one morning with a deep sense of concern. Mike had been really depressed that week and feeling humiliated about what he had done. He was a deacon in our church, and many people looked up to him. He was filled with shame, and I was worried he was going to do something drastic.

When I woke up with a heavy sense of concern, I decided to drive to his apartment to see if any lights were on. I parked next to his work van, and for some reason I felt compelled to get in it and pray for him. Mike owned his own business selling equipment, with thousands of dollars worth of stuff in his van, so I knew it was always locked. But when I checked his van door, it was unlocked. So, I got in the driver's seat and began to pray for him. Afterward I opened my eyes, and noticed his journal sitting on the console.

When Our Biggest Fears Become Reality

Now you know you would have read it too. Come on. You know you would have—and I did. I flipped to the entries he'd written around the time he'd called off our engagement. When I read his words, I came face-to-face with my greatest fear of why a man could never love me. He had written details describing things he was struggling with about my personality, but even worse, about the size of my hips and thighs. He wished I was skinnier.

Now I can't fault him for writing this down. Bless his heart, he never knew I would read it or tell you about it. He was just being honest. If you read my journal, you would probably be appalled with some of the things I say too. But to read that he wanted me to be taller and thinner was worse than the pain of the breakup. I was devastated.

Mike's words opened a deeper wound. You see, I grew up with a father, stepfather, and brothers who looked at pornography. From the time I was a little girl, I found magazines in the bathroom with photos of beautiful women who had perfect bodies. I always feared I would have to be that perfect to be loved. I wasn't, and now my worst fear had come true. After reading Mike's journal, every time I saw a beautiful woman or stood in front of a mirror, doubt whispered, *No man will ever want you. You'll never be good enough.*

Rejection. Betrayal. Abandonment. Abuse. Our greatest fears can become the reality of our worst nightmare. Perhaps you have experienced one or all of them. Maybe your father abandoned you, or your husband cheated on you. Maybe your best friend broke your trust, or your teenage daughter has shut you out. The deep pain we feel as a result of broken relationships can cause us to doubt that we are valuable, that future relationships can be healthy, or that anyone would ever want us. We begin to see ourselves as disposable. Easily replaced. Not good enough.

After Mike and I broke up, I went to my pastor and asked him to help me process the excruciating pain I was feeling. I didn't tell him about the journal. I just talked with him about what had happened. I wanted him to tell me how awful my fiancé was and how I had the right to feel betrayed and deceived. I'll never forget my pastor's words: "Renee, you can't put your hope in a man, you can only put your hope in God. A man's love will always disappoint you."

Honestly, I wanted to throw something at him. I didn't want him to correct me; I wanted him to side with me. I was so confused by his words. *How can you love someone and not put your hope in them?* I wondered. It didn't seem possible or make any sense.

Deep in my heart, though, I knew he was right. I had always put my hope in a man's love. I had struggled with codependency most of my life. I had tried to find my "good enough" in what others thought about me. The wind was knocked out of me, and now I had to face my fear of abandonment head-on. I had to separate myself and my worth from a man's decision to want me or not. I had to hold Mike's words and his preferences up to God's Word.

The promise of God's nearness and the fact that He chose me as His own was the only assurance I could hold on to. It wasn't until God was all I had that I realized He was all I needed. Recovering from the heartbreak of being unwanted and rejected, I began to find my identity and value in who I was in Christ.

Doubt's First Shadow

It's easy to think that if we were taller, prettier, skinnier, smarter, younger, or had all that we wanted, we'd be secure. We think all those things could make us feel like we are good enough. But the truth is, even women who "have it all" still struggle with feeling like they aren't good enough.

The Bible opens with the story of a woman who had everything, yet it wasn't enough. Have you ever wondered why Eve couldn't just be happy and secure with what she had? I mean, the woman had it made: she had the perfect Father, a husband who only had eyes for her, a beautiful garden, no bad hair days (surely there was no humidity in Eden), and no wardrobe problems.

God had established Eve's worth through her value as His child and the crown of His creation. He had given Eve every woman's desire: intimacy, beauty, security, significance, and purpose. But when Satan placed himself between Eve and the light of her Father's love, the first shadow of doubt was cast over a woman's heart.

Satan knew Eve's weakness and tapped into her insecurity of not feeling like she was all she could be—or should be. His questions and suggestions implied that she lacked what she needed to measure up. He told her she could "be" more and "have" more if she'd just seek what God told her to stay away from. The enemy lured Eve into the shadows of doubt by turning her heart away from God and eventually getting her to turn on herself.

God had been more than generous when He told Adam and Eve they could eat from any tree in the garden. The only tree that was off limits was the Tree of the Knowledge of Good and Evil. God even explained why He didn't want them to eat from that tree, for they "would certainly die" (Gen. 2:15–17). His boundaries were designed so Adam and Eve could enjoy the lavish wedding gift He had given to them within the protection of their God-given design.

Satan had a cunning plan to deceive God's children by convincing them to doubt God's character and disobey God's commands. He slithered up close to the woman and asked,

> "Did God really say, 'You must not eat from any tree in the garden'?"
> The woman said to the serpent, "We may eat fruit from the trees in the garden, but God did say, 'You must not eat fruit from the tree that is in the middle of the garden [true], and you must not touch it [not true], or you will die.'"

"You will not surely die," the serpent said to the woman. "For God knows that when you eat from it your eyes will be opened, and you will be like God, knowing good and evil." When the woman saw that the fruit of the tree was good for food [it would fill her] and pleasing to the eye [it would make her happy], and also desirable for gaining wisdom [it would make her powerful and smart], she took some and ate it. She also gave some to her husband, who was with her, and he ate it. (Gen. 3:1–6)

I bet Eve was content with what she had until Satan got her to compare herself to someone who had more. The tempter convinced her that something was missing in her life and that the forbidden fruit would make her "like God." A foolish comparison indeed, but all comparisons are. And don't we do it all the time? *If only I was like her. If only I had a husband like hers. If only my children behaved like hers. . . . If only _____, then I'd feel like I was good enough.*

Paul warns us that those who "measure themselves by themselves and compare themselves with themselves" are not wise (2 Cor. 10:12). Our struggle with comparison will always leave us feeling like we're lacking something. We try to do more and be more, but it's never enough. We still feel insecure and wonder what's wrong with us.

What's Wrong with Me?

Do you ever ask yourself: *What's wrong with me?* One day I noticed how many times I do it. When I can't find my keys, when I am mean to my husband, when someone rejects me, when I'm late for work, when I yell at my kids, when I forget to do something important—the list goes on and on. It dawned on me that day that every time I ask, "What's wrong with me?" I actually tell myself that something is wrong with me.

Then I try to figure out my elusive fault so I can change it, but what I need to change is the way I talk to myself. Because every time I say, "What's wrong with me?" I plant a seed of doubt and convince myself more and more that something is wrong with me.

That is not what God wants me to say to myself, and it's not what He wants you to say to yourself either. However, we have an enemy who loves to cast the shadow of self-doubt over us and get us to focus on all that is wrong with us (real or perceived), instead of anything that is right with us.

Satan is the father of lies; there is no truth in him (John 8:44). He wants us to believe lies that leave us feeling inadequate and unsure of ourselves. The meaning of the word *lie* is "a falsehood with the intent to deceive." Satan intends to deceive us by getting us to take our eyes off of who we are in Christ and focus on our flaws—and then spend our days figuring out how we can hide them. It's what he did with Eve in the garden. In fact, I wonder if Eve might have thought, *What's wrong with me?* when she became aware of her inadequacy.

> Then the eyes of both [Adam and Eve] were opened, and they realized they were naked; so they sewed fig leaves together and made coverings for themselves.
>
> Then the man and his wife heard the sound of the Lord God as he was walking in the garden in the cool of the day, and they hid from the Lord God among the trees of the garden. But the Lord God called to the man, "Where are you?"
>
> He answered, "I heard you in the garden, and I was afraid because I was naked; so I hid." (Gen. 3:7–11)

God asked who had told them they were naked. In other words, "Who told you that something is wrong with you?" By asking this, He acknowledged that there was someone casting shame on them—and it wasn't Him. He wanted them to know they had an enemy whispering lies into their hearts, causing them to move away from Him and from each other.

Do you ever feel like someone is telling you that you can't measure up? That something is wrong with you? It's because sometimes that is what is happening. Sadly, we often believe Satan's lies and live like they are true. Rarely do we stop to ask, "Who is saying these things? Who is causing me to doubt myself? Is it me? Is there something from my past that led me to believe this? Or is it the enemy of my soul disguising his voice as my own?"

Satan's plot is the same for you and me as it was for Eve, but we don't have to go along with him. Instead we can refute his lies and temptations with truth. If we have put our trust in Christ as our Savior, we can stand on the promises of who we are in Him—chosen, holy, and dearly loved (Col. 3:12).

In his book, *Victory Over the Darkness*, Dr. Neil T. Anderson says, "The more you reaffirm who you are in Christ, the more your behavior will begin to reflect your true identity!"[1] Here is a compilation of Scriptures Dr. Anderson's ministry created to remind us of who we are in Christ.

Who I Am in Christ

I am accepted . . .	
John 1:12	I am God's child.
John 15:15	I am a friend of Jesus Christ, as His disciple.
Romans 5:1	I have been justified.
1 Corinthians 6:17	I am united with the Lord, and I am one with Him in spirit.
1 Corinthians 6:19–20	I have been bought with a price and I belong to God.
1 Corinthians 12:27	I am a member of Christ's body.
Ephesians 1:3–8	I have been chosen by God and adopted as His child.
Hebrews 4:14–16	I have direct access to the throne of grace through Jesus Christ.

I am secure . . .	
Romans 8:1–2	I am free from condemnation.
Romans 8:28	I am assured that God works for my good in all circumstances.
Romans 8:31–39	I am free from condemnation. I cannot be separated from God's love.
2 Corinthians 1:21–22	I have been established, anointed, and sealed by God.
Philippians 1:6	I am confident God will complete the good work He started in me.
Philippians 3:20	I am a citizen of heaven.
Colossians 3:1–4	I am hidden with Christ in God.
2 Timothy 1:7	I have been given a spirit of power, love, and a sound mind.
1 John 5:18	I am born of God, and the evil one cannot touch me.

I am significant . . .	
John 15:5	I am a branch of Jesus Christ, the true vine, and a channel of His life.
John 15:16	I have been chosen and appointed to bear fruit.
1 Corinthians 3:16	I am God's temple.
2 Corinthians 5:17–21	I am a minister of reconciliation for God.
Ephesians 2:6	I am seated with Jesus Christ in the heavenly realm.
Ephesians 2:10	I am God's workmanship.
Ephesians 3:12	I may approach God with freedom and confidence.
Philippians 4:13	I can do all things through Christ, who strengthens me.

Testing or Trusting God's Promises

Satan tempted Jesus in the very same way he tempted Eve. In Matthew 4, we read that "After fasting forty days and forty nights, [Jesus] was hungry. The tempter came to him and said, 'If you are the Son of God, tell these stones to become bread'" (vv. 2–3). Satan was tempting Jesus to get His needs met apart from His Father's provision. He also basically said, "If you are who you say you are, then prove your identity through your performance." Instead of giving in, Jesus refuted Satan with truth by answering: "It is written: 'Man shall not live on bread alone, but on every word that comes from the mouth of God'" (v. 4).

Next Satan wanted to see if Jesus would test or trust God's promises. He took Jesus to Jerusalem and had Him stand on the highest point of the temple. "'If you are the Son of God,' he said, 'throw yourself down. For it is written: "He will command his angels concerning you, and they will lift you up in their hands, so that you will not strike your foot against a stone"'" (v. 6). Once again, Jesus knew Satan's intentions. He responded by reminding Himself and the enemy of God's command: "It is also written: 'Do not put the Lord your God to the test'" (v. 7).

Wanting to defeat God's Son, the devil led Jesus to a very high mountain peak so that He could see all the kingdoms of the world and their splendor. "'All this I will give you,' he said, 'if you will bow down and worship me'" (v. 9). Satan is always looking for someone to worship him, but Jesus had had enough. He commanded, "'Away from me, Satan! For it is written: "Worship the Lord your God, and serve him only."' Then the devil left him, and angels came and attended him" (v. 10).

Doubting God's promises makes it hard to trust God's heart. That's why we need to recognize Satan's lies, refute his temptations, and rely on God's Word instead.

His Goodness Makes Me Good Enough

Eve let Satan convince her that her "good enough" could come from something other than what God had promised and provided. By believing Satan's lies, Eve revealed that her heart didn't believe God's truth. Trying to get our "good enough" outside of God's promises and provision will always create insecurity and obstruct our relationship with Him and with other people.

Satan also tried to convince Jesus He could find His "good enough" by seeking position and power apart from what His Father had promised. Yet Jesus didn't let Satan bully Him like Eve did. He used God's Word as His sword and found victory over His enemy. He knew God's Word was the only way to defeat Satan's lies. Jesus trusted His Father's provision and promises because He knew who He was and whose He was. He found His identity and confidence in the words spoken by His Father: "This is my Son, whom I love; with him I am well pleased" (Matt. 3:17).

One day my friend Gary shared on his blog how he had let Satan beat him up with self-doubt. Here is what he wrote:

My daughter Emily got me thinking of one of my bullies. I hate him. He's sneaky and he lies. When I get busy and tired, and especially if I'm discouraged, he starts in. He loves it when there are several things that have to be done at the same time and it's going to be a challenge but I have to get there, and I lack confidence, and fear I won't finish. That's when he starts his bullying. He tells me a very simple, very subtle lie. He doesn't say it out loud, but I sense my soul hears it, and if I'm not careful believes it: "You are what you do. If you fail, then that's who you are."

Funny, when I succeed, that's never who I am; only failure becomes my identity. So, I've decided to come up with two answers to our "You're not good enough—you're not as good as you should be" feeling:

Admit it. Simply say, "You got that right. I'm all wrecked up. You don't know the half of it." There, that settles the performance part. Because even when I succeed, I'm wrecked up.

Get your good enough from Jesus. When you belong to Jesus, you're clothed in His righteousness, forever beloved and accepted, a constant recipient of His steadfast love and grace.

I was slouched over in church one day and my wife Brenda passed me a note: "You belong to the King." She's right. We belong to Him, wrecked up and all. That should matter![2]

The truth is, we are all "wrecked up," but we are loved with reckless abandon by the King of Glory. We may be rejected by man, but we are accepted and adored by our Maker. We may be betrayed and cast aside, but we are chosen and redeemed by our heavenly Father.

Beat Up or Built Up?

One morning I felt beat up by discouragement. My mind was being bullied by thoughts of doubt: I can't do it all! I am not cut out to be a wife, mom, and leader of an organization that ministers to women all around the world! My thoughts were against me and my feelings were too.

As I lay in bed feeling completely inadequate, my radio alarm came on, and my thoughts were interrupted by Twila Paris singing to me. With confident assurance, she spoke truth into my soul. She told me this was not a time for fear, but a time for faith and determination. She told me not to lose my vision or be carried away by my emotions, but to hold on to all that I had hidden in my heart and all that I believed to be true. Then she encouraged me with the most important truth of all: *God is in control.*[3]

I had set my radio to a Christian station the night before, so I would be awakened by encouraging music. As I heard these words, my thoughts were aligned with God's truth. It changed my whole perspective. I went from feeling afraid to feeling determined, from feeling out of control to knowing God is in control.

You and I have the choice to either let doubt beat us up or let God's truth build us up. If we have Christ in us, we have full access to God's power and His promises to live with a confident heart. But it won't just happen because it's possible. We have to take action. Just as I had to tune my radio to encouraging music, we need to get intentional about tuning our thoughts to God's thoughts toward us, every day.

Tuning in to God's Thoughts toward Us

In the same way a radio has AM and FM frequencies, so do our thoughts. They are either AM (against me) thoughts or FM (for me) thoughts. Many times we can be our worst critics, and we have a lot of AM thoughts. We also have an enemy who is completely against us. He is jealous of God's glory in us and threatened by the beauty that lies within the heart of a woman whose identity is secure. That is why he attacks our confidence. He knows if he can paralyze us with self-doubt and insecurity we will never live up to the full potential of who we are and what we have in Christ.

Now, we don't need to be afraid of our enemy. The One who is in us is greater than the one who is against us. However, we do need to be aware of his schemes and ready to stand against them. Peter tells us how:

> Keep your mind clear, and be alert. Your opponent the devil is prowling around like a roaring lion as he looks for someone to devour. Be firm in the faith and resist him, knowing that other believers throughout the world are going through the same kind of suffering. (1 Pet. 5:8–9 GW)

We need to keep our minds clear by asking Jesus to replace the clutter of insecurity, pride, and Satan's lies with the clarity of His truth. This is crucial, because the battlefield is our minds. Our enemy knows if he can influence the way we think, then our thoughts will determine how we feel, and our feelings will shape how we live. But we're not going to let that happen anymore. Instead, we're going to get into God's Word and get God's Word into us so that as we rely on His life in us, He can shape the way we think, which will change the way we feel and positively transform the way we live.

Think → Feel → Live

Peter also said we need to be alert. The best way to do that is by slowing down to listen to our thoughts. If our thoughts are against us, our feelings will be too. When you get that "not good enough" feeling, stop and ask God what triggered your thoughts and made you start turning toward the shadow of doubt. Then compare your thoughts about that situation to God's thoughts. Do they match? If not, look for a promise in God's Word to replace the lie that has filled your heart with doubt. Here are some AM and FM thoughts to help you get started:

- When doubt comes **against me**, saying I'm not good enough, I will rely on the truth that God is **for me!** He says I'm fearfully and wonderfully made; all of His works are wonderful and I am one of them (Ps. 139:14).

- When doubt comes **against me**, saying I'm weak and all alone, I will live in the truth that God is **for me!** I can be strong and courageous because the Lord my God is with me. He will never leave me nor forsake me (Deut. 31:6).

- When doubt comes **against me**, saying I shouldn't get my hopes up because I'll only be disappointed, I will depend on the truth that God is **for me**! He has plans for my life that are filled with purpose and hope (Jer. 29:11).

- When doubt comes **against me**, saying I'm not good enough for a certain role or position, I will remember that God is **for me**! He says I am His masterpiece, created to be new in Christ so that I could do good things He planned long ago. (Eph. 2:10).

- When doubt comes **against me**, saying nobody really loves me, I will hold on to the truth that God is **for me**! He loves me so much that He gave His only Son to live and die for me, and He chose me to be adopted into His family (John 3:16; Eph. 1:4–5).

- When doubt comes **against me**, saying I can't do something because it's too hard, I will cling to the truth that God is **for me**! He says I can do all things through Christ who strengthens me (Phil. 4:13).

From the minute we wake up, we need to tune in and listen to God's thoughts toward us. Instead of letting doubt come against you, start every day relying on God's power and living in the security of His promises. And remember, it won't just happen because it's possible; you have to take action.

So, write these AM/FM thoughts on index cards (you'll find more in chapter 12), tape them to your mirror, take them to work, put them on your desk, stick them on your refrigerator or in your car, and read them out loud as you walk around your house. The more you hear God's Word, the more you will believe it, rely on it, and live like it is true!

Let's keep turning our hearts and minds away from the shadows of doubt caused by rejection as we accept, believe, and live in the promise that we are valuable, sought after, delighted in, and chosen!

Although people's preferences will change, God's desire for us won't. Others might not think we're good enough, but God always will. And even if someone decides they don't desire us anymore, God most certainly does! The truth is, when we belong to Jesus we are loved and accepted forever. We are covered in His goodness, and it's His goodness that makes us good enough!

Just in case you are wondering what ever happened between Mike and me, we're happily married—to other people. But we attended each other's weddings and celebrated the redeeming work God has done in our hearts and in our lives, together and apart.

Praying God's Promises

Lord, thank You that in Christ I'm chosen, holy, and dearly loved. I love knowing I am a crown of splendor in my Lord's hand, a royal diadem in the hand of my God. Whenever someone rejects me, heal my hurting heart with the promise that You will never leave me or forsake me. When I'm tempted to find my significance and security apart from Your provision and promises, help me resist Satan's lies and temptations and stand firm in my faith. When insecurity threatens to take me captive, I will remember that Christ set me free, and not allow myself to be burdened again by a yoke of slavery.

Holy Spirit, remind me every day that such confidence as this is mine through Christ—not that I am competent in myself to claim anything for myself, but competence comes from Him. I have been given fullness in Christ, who is the

Head over every power and authority. I choose to believe His goodness makes me good enough! In Jesus' powerful name I pray, Amen.

See Colossians 3:12; Isaiah 62:3; Deuteronomy 31:6; 1 Peter 5:9; Galatians 5:1; 2 Corinthians 3:4–5; Colossians 2:10.

Reflection and Discussion Questions

1. What area of your life—as a woman, mom, wife, friend, daughter, housekeeper, professional, leader, etc.—do you currently struggle with most in believing you are good enough?

2. Has anyone ever said or done anything to make you feel rejected? If so, describe what happened and what that circumstance led you to believe about yourself.

3. Go back and review the "Who I Am in Christ" chart. Highlight verses that speak to your heart most about believing you are accepted, secure, or significant. Choose seven of the verses/promises and write them on note cards. Read and pray out loud a different one each day this week.

4. Reread the stories of Eve and of Jesus being tempted. What are the common lies Satan tried to get them to believe?

5. What were the different ways Eve and Jesus responded to Satan's lies?

6. Do you recognize Satan as a spiritual bully who wants to intimidate and defeat you? How will you take what you know now and prepare yourself for the daily battles when he tries to steal your confidence as a child of God?

7. What are one or two AM (against me) thoughts you are currently dealing with? What FM (for me) thoughts from God's promises will you replace them with?

7

When Doubt Whispers
"I'm Such a Failure"

One reason we doubt God's love is that we have an adversary who uses every little offense to accuse us of being good-for-nothings. But your advocate Jesus Christ is more powerful than your adversary. He has cancelled the debt of your sins past, present, and future. No matter what you do or how you fail, God has no reason not to love you and accept you completely.

Dr. Neil T. Anderson[1]

I admire, maybe even envy, people who are not afraid to fail. You know those people: they see personal setbacks as another goal to conquer. They don't even consider it a defeat when they blow it. I wish I was that kind of person, but I am not always so courageous in the face of failure. Failure can be painful and embarrassing. Sometimes it makes me want to give up, mainly on myself.

That's exactly how I felt one afternoon when I let the overwhelming stress of being a mom bring on feelings of frustration and failure. It had been a hard day, running too many errands with two small children. My son Joshua, who was three at the time, didn't understand why we couldn't buy every toy his hands could touch. He kept getting in and out of the grocery cart and whining when I tried to stop him. Hoping to escape my misery, I headed to the checkout line, only to encounter more begging for candy bars and bubble gum. I was tempted to ask the cashier at what age children learn to be content.

Obviously I was doing something wrong. The other moms I knew seemed like they were enjoying themselves. Their children listened when they said "no." They even dressed their kids in matching outfits and adorned themselves with attitudes of grace and wisdom. I wondered how in the world they pulled it off with a smile. I could barely get a shower, get my kids dressed, and get us out the door before lunch.

As soon as we got home that afternoon, I rushed the boys through snack time and put them down for an early nap. No bedtime songs or stories. Instead, I headed for the craft box, where I searched for a piece of pink construction paper so I could write "I QUIT" on it. I had decided to turn in my pink slip when my husband got home from work.

Well, I couldn't find any pink construction paper, but I was determined to do something to make myself feel better. I was tempted to eat a gallon of ice cream, but instead I pulled out an article I had promised to edit for a friend. At least I could accomplish one thing that day—and maybe even get some appreciation for it. Little did I know, God was about to accomplish so much more than that. He was about to change my perspective as a mom and especially as a child of God.

Failure Doesn't Have to Be Fatal

My friend's article referenced Zig Ziglar's book *Raising Positive Kids in a Negative World*, where Ziglar shares a story about Andrew Carnegie. The wealthiest man in America in the early 1900s, Carnegie employed more than forty-two millionaires. One day, a reporter asked Carnegie how he helped these men become so valuable that he would pay them that much money. Carnegie explained that "men are developed the same way gold is mined. When gold is mined, several tons of dirt must be moved to get an ounce of gold, but one doesn't go into the mine looking for dirt, one goes in looking for gold, and the more he looks for the more he finds."[2] Zig Ziglar used this story as an illustration, challenging parents to take their focus off their children's mistakes and look for the good in them.

I felt like such a failure. Focused on all that was wrong with my children and me, I was buried deep in the dirt of discouragement and defeat. I was deeply disappointed in myself and convinced God was just as disappointed in me. I no longer had any desire to edit the article, so I put it aside and pulled out my journal.

Filling blank pages with scribbled thoughts, I wrote: *I hate who I have become. I'm such a horrible mom. Why didn't someone tell me how hard this was going to be? I'm frustrated with my kids and myself. I have no patience and I don't know what I am doing! I feel guilty all the time. I couldn't wait to be a mom and now I want to quit. I wish I had a gold miner in my life who could see something good in me.*

Just as I finished writing that sentence, I sensed God whispering to me: *Renee, I am that gold miner. You are the one who is so critical of yourself. You are the one who focuses on your mistakes and beats yourself up with accusation and condemnation. Those are not My thoughts. I see the gold of*

My image, woven into your heart when I created you. I want to bring it to the surface so others can see it too.

The thought that God wasn't focused on the mistakes I was making comforted my heart, although I wasn't sure how He could see anything good in me. I wondered if it was really God speaking. Were those thoughts consistent with His character and what He said in the Bible? I thought about stories and Scriptures where God didn't allow someone's failure to define them or hold them back from being used by Him. Stories of people like Gideon, the man who hid in a winepress like a wimp—until God called him a mighty warrior and helped him become one.

I also thought about Simon Peter, one of Jesus' closest friends. When Jesus asked the disciples, "Who do you say I am?" it was Simon who declared, "You are the Messiah, Son of the living God." Upon hearing those words, Jesus gave him the name Peter, which means "rock," and then told him "on this rock I will build my church" (Matt. 16:16–18). But Peter didn't always live up to his new name. His biggest failure came the night of Jesus' arrest, when Peter denied he even knew Him, three times.

Jesus knew Peter would fail Him, but Peter's past and future failures weren't fatal. They didn't determine how Jesus saw Peter, or the potential Jesus saw in Peter. It was Peter's faith in Christ as Messiah and his love for the Son of God that, despite his obvious shortcomings, gave him potential to be used by God.

Failure Doesn't Get the Final Say

It was almost as if I realized for the first time how very critical I had become—not only of my kids, but of myself. I was letting my failures have the final say about who I was and what

I could do. But God offered me the same grace and mercy He'd given Gideon and Peter.

God saw beyond who I was to who I could become. Knowing this was His perspective gave me the confidence to believe that I didn't have to stay in this hard place. I didn't have to let my failure define me. That day, I started letting God have the final say as my Father as I learned to better understand His perspective of me as His child.

Don't we all struggle with feeling like a failure in one area of our lives or another? For some, it's our past. Our childhood was not what we thought or hoped it would be. Or we've made devastating choices we wish we could erase. Maybe it's our career. We were overlooked for a promotion at work or a position at church, or we're not using the valuable education we worked so hard to gain. Maybe we're not married yet, and that feels like a failure as everyone around us has moved on to the next phase of life. Or we can't have children and wonder if God thinks we're just not cut out for parenthood.

Some of us feel like we're too young or too old to make a difference. Perhaps we don't feel competent to face the future with possible health or financial challenges. Being an adult child brings lots of opportunities to fail. It can be hard to be as available as our aging or long-distance parents want or need us to be.

Sometimes it's not the big things—it's the smaller, everyday things. How often do you hear doubt whisper, *You're such a failure*, when you make a dumb mistake, say something you regret, argue with someone you love, let a friend down, dishonor your husband, or fall into a pattern of sin? How often do you beat yourself up with accusing internal dialogue, saying things like, *I always do that. I keep saying I'm sorry, but I'll never change. I'm constantly disappointing someone.*

When our thoughts heap condemning statements like these on us, we get buried in discouragement and defeat. Failure gets the final say. We become our own worst critic, and once again Satan loves it. Whether you are saying these things to yourself or you're repeating what someone else has said, once again they are exactly what the enemy wants you to believe.

It's a downward spiral that becomes so familiar it's almost easier to keep letting Satan have the final say instead of taking time to find out what God says. But we need to remember that accusation doesn't come from God; it comes from our accuser. Scripture assures us that he will be completely defeated, but until then, he accuses us before God day and night (Rev. 12:10).

Letting Accusation Lead Us to Jesus

Accusing is what Satan does best, but instead of believing his accusations, we need to let them lead us straight to Jesus so He can have the final say. One day, God showed me that I could use Satan's schemes to work for me instead of against me. I was reading a story in the Bible of a woman caught committing adultery. She was taken to Jesus by her accusers, who hoped He would condemn her, but the opposite happened:

> At dawn he [Jesus] appeared again in the temple courts, where all the people gathered around him, and he sat down to teach them. The teachers of the law and the Pharisees brought in a woman caught in adultery. They made her stand before the group and said to Jesus, "Teacher, this woman was caught in the act of adultery. In the Law Moses commanded us to stone such women. Now what do you say?" They were using this question as a trap, in order to have a basis for accusing him. (John 8:2–6)

These men were setting a trap so they could have a basis for accusing Jesus. I have a feeling they had also set a trap to have a basis for accusing this woman too. Scripture tells us she was "caught in the act of adultery," but how did they catch her in bed with a man who wasn't her husband? And where was this man when they took her to Jesus to be stoned?

Setting traps is exactly what Satan does. He lures us into wanting something, and then he turns it around and accuses us on the basis of the very thing he enticed us with. Take, for instance, if we are trying to overcome a struggle such as losing weight or stopping emotional eating. The enemy will whisper to us that we "deserve" that chocolate cake. He'll remind us how we've had a stressful week and made so many sacrifices. He'll then convince us that "surely one piece won't hurt."

We'll eat one, and then another. The next day we regret it, but then we're feeling down and start craving more, so we go back and eat cake until the whole thing is gone. Then we get on the scale and feel completely defeated because we gained back the five pounds we worked so hard to lose. Immediately the accuser's voice of condemnation beats us up, telling us we are a failure because we have no discipline or self-control.

Maybe eating isn't your struggle. Take this same scenario and insert the temptation of gossiping, excessive spending, watching a movie with scenes you don't need to see, or any other thing that tempts you. How many times has the enemy used a little distraction to lead you into a pattern of destruction and then condemned you for it? We see this in the garden with Eve and in our own lives. Do you listen to his accusations, or do you listen to the voice of truth? Let's see how Jesus responded to the accusers in this woman's story:

> But Jesus bent down and started to write on the ground with his finger. When they kept on questioning him, he straightened up and said to them, "Let any one of you who is without sin

be the first to throw a stone at her." Again he stooped down and wrote on the ground. (John 8:6–8)

Jesus simply bent down and wrote on the ground. The text doesn't tell us what He wrote. I have always imagined Jesus writing out the Ten Commandments, since the men had mentioned that Moses' law commanded them to stone her. Perhaps Jesus wanted them to look at all of the commandments, not just the one she had broken. When He stood up, Jesus challenged her accusers to examine their own sins to see if any of them were without fault. He knew the answer, that "there is no one righteous, not even one . . . for all have sinned and fall short of the glory of God" (Rom. 3:10, 23).

He Stoops Down to Make Me Great

When Jesus stooped down to write a second time, I wonder what He wrote then. Again, we don't know for certain, but perhaps Jesus wrote redemptive words like grace, forgiveness, and mercy. I wonder if Jesus replaced the weight of the law with the liberty of His love. Whatever He wrote, something radical happened. Everyone dropped their stones and went away.

> At this, those who heard began to go away one at a time, the older ones first, until only Jesus was left, with the woman still standing there. Jesus straightened up and asked her, "Woman, where are they? Has no one condemned you?"
> "No one, sir," she said.
> "Then neither do I condemn you," Jesus declared. "Go now and leave your life of sin." (John 8:9–11)

In the presence of Jesus, the woman's accusers walked away. He dismissed them one by one, until He was the only one left standing. Her failure didn't get the final say; Jesus did.

Although He knew she had sinned by committing adultery, Jesus also knew that her sin was not *who* she was. It was what she had done. When Jesus stooped down, He helped this woman stand up and face her failures in the light of His love. Jesus took what her accusers meant for evil and used it for good. He wanted her setback to help her step forward.

The day I got buried in my failures as a mom, I told God I wanted to change. I didn't want to keep living in defeat and give up my legacy as a mom. I remember choking out the words, "I can't do this, God. I don't know how." In that place of surrender, I felt like God was bending down on His knees before me, looking into my eyes and speaking to my heart: *You are right, Renee. In your own strength and through your own perspective, you cannot do this. But I am here with you. I will help you.*

As I think about this woman's failure, and mine, I am reminded of Psalm 18:35, "You have given me your shield of victory. Your right hand supports me; your help has made me great" (NLT). God wants to give us a new starting place. He sees beyond who we are to who we are becoming.

When you acknowledge to Him that you've made a mistake—or a big mess called sin—God wants to come to your rescue and give you victory. He wants to sustain you and show you that with His grace, mercy, and help, you can use your setbacks to help get back on your feet again, and find your confidence in Christ by believing what He says about you.

There Is No Condemnation

This woman experienced the power of living in God's promise, "There is now no condemnation for those who are in Christ Jesus" (Rom. 8:1), and so can you. Although you may condemn yourself for your failures, Jesus never will. You may even try to make up for your sins, but you can't—and you don't have to.

> [If] you belong to him, the power of the life-giving Spirit has freed you from the power of sin that leads to death. The law of Moses was unable to save us because of the weakness of our sinful nature. So God did what the law could not do. He sent his own Son in a body like the bodies we sinners have. And in that body God declared an end to sin's control over us by giving his Son as a sacrifice for our sins. He did this so that the just requirement of the law would be fully satisfied for us, who no longer follow our sinful nature but instead follow the Spirit. (Rom. 8:2–4 NLT)

Whatever you have done, or will do, God still loves you and He forgives you. Many of us are familiar with John 3:16, "For God so loved the world that he gave his one and only Son, that whoever believes in him shall not perish but have eternal life." Yet how many of us have stopped reading there and missed the promise that there is no condemnation when we belong to Jesus? "For God did not send his Son into the world to condemn the world, but to save the world through him. Whoever believes in him is not condemned" (vv. 17–18).

Just as the woman was brought to Jesus by her accusers after being caught in sin, God wants the same for you. Although at one time "you were alienated from God," and were even His enemy, now "he has reconciled you by Christ's physical body through death to present you holy in his sight, without blemish and free from accusation" (Col. 1:21–22).

What about Conviction?

God's Spirit will convict you, but His heart will never condemn you. How do we know if we are hearing the voice of condemnation that comes from our accuser, or the voice of conviction that comes from God? I once heard a pastor describe the difference between conviction and condemnation. Condemnation sweeps across our thoughts with generalized statements such as, *You're such a failure, You're so hypocritical*, or *You can never be counted on.* That is the accuser. His tone is condemning, questioning, and confusing. His accusations lead to guilt and shame.

The Holy Spirit's conviction will be specific. He will reveal a sinful action or attitude and instruct us on what we need to do to right the wrong, whether it's restoring a broken relationship or returning something that isn't ours. He'll give us steps we need to take to change our behavior or attitude.

- Instead of *You're such a failure as a [wife, mom, daughter, friend]*, the Spirit might say, *You were really critical the way you talked to _____ (your husband, child, parent, etc.). You need to say you are sorry and ask for forgiveness. Then tell them something that will build them up instead of tearing them down.*

- Instead of *You're so hypocritical*, the Spirit might say, *You judge others for gossiping, but you are doing the same thing when you talk about your neighbor at work. Tomorrow at lunch break, apologize for what you said and share a few things that are positive about her.*

- Instead of *You can never be counted on*, the Spirit might say, *You didn't keep your promise to go see your mom today. Call her to apologize and maybe set up a lunch date for this weekend.*

God uses conviction lovingly, to show us our sin and lead our hearts to repentance. He does this to draw us away from destructive behavior that hinders our relationship with Him and with others. His desire is to bring us out of the darkness of sin and back into the light, so that we can walk with Him in the freedom of forgiveness and the confidence of His love.

Failing Forward

We are all going to fail and fall short of our expectations and others'. But if our steps "are established by the LORD, and He delights in [our] way, when [we] fall, [we] will not be hurled headlong, because the LORD is the One who holds [our] hand" (Ps. 37:23–24 NASB). A confident woman trusts this truth. Even when she falls, she doesn't stay down. Instead, she reaches for God's hand and rises again (Prov. 24:16).

God has been challenging me to live out these truths again and again lately. I keep falling short and He keeps reminding me that I am a work in progress, and as I rely on Christ in me, I am moving forward even when I have a setback. In fact, He is giving me a little push these days to fail forward.

Failing forward . . . after I criticize my husband and realize I failed to honor my man, again. Instead, I've added to an already stressful day for the husband and father who just brought home groceries.

Failing forward . . . after I let myself be too busy to take time to sit down and visit with a neighbor who stopped by unexpectedly to pick something up this afternoon.

Failing forward . . . after I shoot harsh words across the room to shush my son, who announced the yogurt in our otherwise-empty refrigerator was expired—after I just opened the large container of perfectly good yogurt, ate some, and served a bowl to his brother for a snack.

Failing forward . . . after I miss my deadline again and have to ask for another extension.

Failing forward . . . after I miss my flight and have to cancel plans with a friend who drove two hours to meet me at the airport for lunch during a long layover.

Failing forward . . . after telling my mom I can't fulfill some big promises I made to her.

Failing forward . . . after I tell God that writing a book is too stinkin' hard and I can't do it because I don't have what it takes.

When we disappoint God or other people, it can automatically make us feel like a failure. This reinforces Satan's lies and destroys our confidence. Fearing failure can distort our perspective and keep us focused on the fear of failing again. Instead, we need to ask God if there is something we need to do differently.

One of the main themes of the Bible is overcoming failure. Throughout Scripture we see that failure is sometimes caused by disobedience (Num. 14:40–45), sin (Josh. 7:3–12), lack of faith (Matt. 17:15–21), not following God's ways (2 Chron. 28:1–5), lack of counting the cost (Luke 14:28–29), unbelief (Heb. 4:6), and wrong motives (James 4:3). But even when wrongdoing causes our failure, it doesn't have to be fatal or final. When we fail or feel like a failure, we need to ask ourselves some questions:

- Did I do something wrong or make a bad decision that led to this failure?
- Am I acting independently of God?
- Is there anything I am not doing to fulfill a commitment I made?
- Did I pray about this or just do it because I wanted to?

- Was I responsible for the outcome?
- Did I overcommit myself in agreeing to do this?
- Is God using this to refine my character?

I recently let someone down, and I felt terrible about it. I was going through a season of constant stress and health challenges with both of my parents. I also had personal health problems but didn't know it; I just thought I was tired, so I kept pushing through. When I found out how much I had let this person down, I knew I had a choice. I could feel like a total failure or I could fail forward.

I knew I had given this person and this project all that I had to give, but my best wasn't good enough. I had let some important details fall through the cracks. I hadn't communicated some of my limitations. Instead of taking it personally, I asked God to help me find lessons I could learn from it. Then I wrote a letter apologizing and explaining what had happened. I asked for forgiveness, and she graciously gave it to me.

We have to accept that we are going to disappoint people, especially if we are seeking to please God. Sometimes we need to lower our expectations of ourselves and lighten our overloaded list of commitments. We also need to stop the habit of beating ourselves up with so much critical thinking. What are we doing, talking to a child of God the way we talk to ourselves? When criticism comes and we have done our best, we can rest in knowing God is pleased. If we didn't do our best, we need to give ourselves grace and try again by failing forward.

Becoming

Although it seems contradictory, failure can help us become the confident women God created us to be. It can make us stronger and better—if we go to God for help. Failure produces wisdom when we ask for it and maturity when we learn from it. Failure pushes us to do more than we think we can and try other methods of doing things when one way doesn't work. Failure can be hurtful, but it can also be beneficial.

I know failure can shape us and give us unlikely confidence—because that's what happened the day I felt like such a failure as a mom. Remember how I wanted to quit? The day I hit rock bottom and cried out for help, God showed me His perspective of me as His child. He then challenged me to look for ways to have that same perspective as a mom, to see beyond who my children were to who they could become. To love them and lead them toward the heart of God.

I thought about the difference it could make for my kids to know I was intent on finding the gold in them, but I wasn't sure what that would look like. Then I remembered how my husband and I had tried to teach Joshua the importance of character, but he wasn't interested. As I thought about the gold I wanted to find in my children, character traits flooded my mind. I wrote down two categories: golden attitudes and golden actions.

I listed traits like kindness, obedience, honesty, and thankfulness, and then wrote down Bible verses for each trait. I also listed not-so-golden traits like anger, selfishness, whining, arguing, and discontentment. Those represented the dirt that buries the gold. The next day, I was so inspired I created a character chart and made gold nuggets by balling up foil and spray-painting it gold. I told my husband about it, and we decided to focus on a different trait each week while looking for ways to live them in our everyday lives.

We talked about how we showed patience, used kind words, took initiative, and so forth each day, and incorporated the corresponding Bible verses into prayers for our family and others. When we saw Joshua displaying a golden action or attitude, we gave him a gold nugget and set up a system so he could save and redeem nuggets for special treats or family activities. These became tangible reminders of God's promise to reward us for following Him. As I read Bible stories with my boys, I looked for lessons in the lives of people who showed good or bad character. The new perspective God gave me for parenting started to shape my prayers as I asked Him to mold our characters to look more like His.

Our home changed the week I was ready to give up, and it has never been the same. Thirteen years later, mining for gold in the heart of our children has become a reality. We even published a "Mining for Gold in the Heart of Your Child Character Chart."[3]

I'm so glad God used my mess to speak His message to my heart and eventually allowed me to share it with other struggling moms. More than anything, He taught me that my failures don't have to be fatal; if I let them, they can help me become more like Him.

Will you let your failures lead you to Jesus? Will you do the best you can and allow His strength to perfect your weaknesses? And when you fail, will you choose to fail forward?

In Christ, you are a woman who is becoming all God created you to be. Trusting in His power and relying on His promises, you are a woman who is growing—a woman who is becoming more like Jesus each day. A woman who is not perfect, but who is surrendering to God's perfect power and love at work in her.

Every time you fail to be the woman God calls you to be, or the woman you expect yourself to be, let God remind you of the progress you've made. Even though you may not be quite who you want to be, you are not who you used to be! You get that much closer to who you are meant to be every time you *fail forward*.

Praying God's Promises

Lord, thank You that my failures never get the final say—You do! You say there is no condemnation for those who are in Christ Jesus, and my life is hidden in Him. When my heart or my enemy tries to condemn me, I will have confidence, believing that I will receive from You anything I ask according to Your Word and Your will, as I obey Your commands and seek what pleases You.

Because my steps are established by You, Lord, I will believe that You delight in me even when I fail or fall. When I have a setback, I will get back up again because You give me Your shield of victory and Your right hand sustains me; Your help makes me great. Thank You for Your grace that is sufficient for me. I choose to rely on Your promise to perfect Your power through my weakness, so that Christ's power may rest on me. In Jesus' name I pray, Amen.

See Romans 8:1; Colossians 3:3; 1 John 3:21–22; Psalms 37:23–24; 18:35; 2 Corinthians 12:9.

Reflection and Discussion Questions

1. On a scale of 1–10 (with 1 being "very little" and 10 being "a whole lot"), how often do you hear doubt whisper, *You're such a failure?* Do you ever hear accusing internal dialogue saying things like, *You always do that; You keep saying you're sorry, but you'll never change;* or *You're constantly disappointing someone?*
2. Do your failures ever feel final or fatal? If so, describe a time when you failed and how you let it define you.
3. Jesus knew Peter would fail Him, yet He still saw beyond who Peter was to who he could become. How does it make you feel to know the same is true in your life? Write down an area where you are feeling like a failure

or are afraid you might fail, and ask Jesus to help you confidently fail forward even if you have a setback.

4. Have you ever felt like you fell into one of Satan's traps? How will you let his accusations lead you to Jesus in the future?

5. What is the difference between condemnation and conviction?

6. Describe a time when you felt condemned (by yourself or someone else). What would the difference have been if you had processed the situation through the filter of conviction instead? What steps can you take next time to usher in restoration instead of condemnation?

7. "Every time you fail to be the woman God calls you to be, or the woman you expect yourself to be, let God remind you of the progress you've made. Even though you may not be quite who you want to be, you are not who you used to be! You get that much closer to who you are meant to be every time you *fail forward*" (pg. 132). List your personal "failing forward" statements. Carry them with you this week and share them with a friend!

8

When Doubt Whispers "I Don't Have Anything Special to Offer"

Don't ask yourself what the world needs. Ask yourself what makes you come alive, and then go do that. Because what the world needs is people who have come alive.

Harold Thurman Whitman

I sat there dreading my turn to talk. The facilitator of our "team-building activity" had asked our group of eight to answer two questions: "What do you love to do?" and "If finances were unlimited and failure was unlikely, what would be your dream?"

I started praying we would run out of time before it was my turn to talk. But just in case I had to answer, I listened to everyone else describe their dreams, hoping to get some ideas. One woman said she loved leading people and dreamed of becoming the first female president of the United States. Another friend said she loved to sing and always wanted to be in a Christian rock band.

I knew I was in trouble. I was thirty-two years old at the time, and didn't know what I liked to do or what my dreams were. When it was my turn to answer, the group listened as I stumbled over my words before finally admitting I didn't have a dream. Insecurity whispered: *That's because dreams are for confident people who have something special to offer, and you don't.*

Feeling like a third grader living in a grown woman's body, I wondered, *Do I want to be a nurse, a schoolteacher, or a movie star? Who am I? What do I like to do? What do I have to offer?*

Up to that point in my life, I'd never taken time to ask or answer those kinds of questions. Instead, I had tried to be who others wanted, expected, or needed me to be. I was fairly good at it. But I also suffered symptoms common to those with the "disease to please." I lived with an uneasy feeling of just not being happy, whether at home, at work, or in ministry. I was also a constant candidate for burnout and never felt like I measured up to other women.

Breaking Free from the Comparison Trap

From the time I was in junior high, I didn't really like who I was. I know a lot of us didn't like ourselves at that age, but we all desperately wanted others to like us. At that point, many of us compared ourselves to those around us, observed who was liked most, and tried to be like the popular people.

When we fall into the comparison trap, it's easy to feel like we don't have as much to offer as others do. And it doesn't just happen when we are teenagers. I believe comparison is one of woman's worst enemies.

Comparison leaves us insecure, confused, and discontent. My friend Genia summed it up well when she told me, "Every time I compare myself with someone else, I can never measure up because I am comparing my insides with their outsides." She is so right. We compare how we feel inadequate on the inside with someone who looks like they have it all together on the outside. Then we try to polish our outsides, hoping that will make us feel better on the inside, but it never does.

Comparison causes us to compete with each other, but no one wins. God never intended for us to compete with each other; He wants us to complete one another, celebrating and encouraging each other's strengths while discovering who He created us to be. Paul explains why in 1 Corinthians 12:18–20:

> But in fact God has placed the parts in the body, every one of them, just as he wanted them to be. If they were all one part, where would the body be? As it is, there are many parts, but one body.

The only way you can break free from the comparison trap is to embrace the reason you are who you are. "[You are] God's masterpiece. He has created [you] anew in Christ Jesus, so [you] can do the good things he planned for [you] long ago" (Eph. 2:10 NLT). You do things the way you do because it is part of your unique, God-shaped purpose.

Getting to Know the Real Me

Later that day, after our "team-building activity," the facilitator encouraged me to ask God what His dreams were for my life and spend time getting to know myself better. She also suggested I read books on personalities and spiritual gifts. I didn't want to stay in that confusing place of not knowing who I was or what I had to offer, so I took her advice and began a process of getting to know the "real me" who had gotten buried under the busyness of life and people-pleasing.

As I read books about different temperaments and personality traits, I started to recognize what I liked, strengths that came naturally to me, and what I needed emotionally to encourage my heart. Instead of seeking to become more like women I admired, I realized there was a reason I was who I was, with my passionate preferences and mixed bag of emotions. While reading these books, for the first time I felt like someone understood me. I also started to sense God wanted to use the unique way He made me to shape my heart for ministry.

Isn't it easy to completely neglect our dreams and desires to meet the needs of everyone around us and call it self-sacrifice? It sounds godly, but in doing so we risk shutting down a place in our soul where God's dreams and gifts are waiting to be revealed. It's not self-seeking but God-seeking to intentionally get to know and become the woman God created you to be.

So I'm wondering: have you ever taken time to think about what you like to do? What makes your heart come alive? How would you fill your free time if you had no fears or insecurities?

Maybe when you hear the words "free time" you think, *I don't have any.* If so, please give yourself permission to take time to get to know the "real you." I know all of life is screaming for your time, but instead of giving your divided attention to many good things, commit to setting aside time each week to walk through the process of finding God's things for you.

A confident woman wants to know who God created her to be. She is comfortable saying "no" to some things so that she can say "yes" to living the life God wants her to live. She is intentional and secure about pursuing the spiritual purpose God has for her. In this chapter, I want to help you do just that. We are going to look at how God created you with a unique personality, God-given passions, and abilities that can help others, as well as spiritual giftedness and life experiences that prepare and equip you for His plans and purposes.

If you are reading this book with a friend or a group of friends, great! If not, I want to encourage you to consider going through this chapter alongside someone else, whether it be a friend, a coworker, or your husband. Their insights will be valuable. Also, there are a few things you will need: a Bible, a pen, a journal, and a willingness to be very honest with yourself and God. You will also need the important commodity of time, so be sure to block some out.

Uniquely You

When God looks at you, He sees someone He loves. In Isaiah 43:4, God says, "You are precious and honored in my sight . . . and I love you." When God looks at you, He also sees someone He knows. David said in Psalm 139:1, "You have searched me, LORD, and you know me." You are not just one of millions of others, but are uniquely you. You are God's prized possession, a valued treasure of great worth.

Your personality is one aspect that makes you uniquely you. Your personality is your most natural way of doing things. You have strengths, and you have what I call "relational challenges." God deliberately gave you the personality He wanted you to have so He could impact certain people through your life.

In her book *Personality Plus*, Florence Littauer describes four personality types.[1] This book was a key that opened the door to me discovering and valuing the unique way God made me. I have included a summary for you that I compiled from the writings of Florence Littauer. See if you can identify which personality traits best describe you.

Phlegmatic: Desires PEACE

Needs times of quiet, reduced stress, feeling of worth, respect

Strengths	Relational Challenges
Calm	Stubborn
Adds balance	Uninvolved
Witty	Procrastinates
Low-key	Unenthusiastic
Considerate	Hard to motivate
Reliable	Denial
Makes peace	Careless

Choleric: Desires CONTROL

Needs appreciation for achievements, opportunity for leadership, participation in decisions

Strengths	Relational Challenges
Problem solver	Opinionated
Decisive	Workaholic tendency
Natural leader	Usurps authority
Good organizer	Insensitive
Task oriented	Arrogant
High energy	Manipulative
Excels in crisis	Has a hard time admitting her faults
Confident	

Sanguine: Desires FUN

Needs interaction, affection, approval, attention

Strengths	Relational Challenges
Loves people	Emotional
Friendly	Dislikes schedules
Exciting	Makes excuses
Humorous	Gets bored easily

Sanguine: Desires FUN	
Needs interaction, affection, approval, attention	
Strengths	**Relational Challenges**
Charming	Loses track of time
Creative	Takes on too much
Thrives on activity	Easily distracted
Great storyteller	

Melancholy: Desires PERFECTION	
Needs understanding, stability, support, space, silence	
Strengths	**Relational Challenges**
Works well alone	Easily depressed
Planner	Lacks spontaneity
Organized	Naively idealistic
Accurate	Thrifty to extremes
Intuitive	Doesn't do well under pressure
Fair	Perfectionist
Creative	Hard to please
Empathetic	Discontent
Good with numbers	

When I read these traits for the first time, I felt like I had multiple personalities. In actuality, most of us are a unique blend of two of these personality types. As I prayed through them and asked God to give me the confidence to be my most natural self, I saw that I had two predominant blends. We all have God-given desires that drive us, and that's okay.

I also began to understand we have God-given emotional needs. When those needs are left completely unmet, we become depleted and tend to operate primarily out of our weaknesses. We all have strengths, and when surrendered to Christ, we become more like Him as we become more like our true selves. As I have said before, none of us is perfect, but we are wonderfully made—just as God planned.

If God knows you, has a purpose for you, and loves you just the way He made you, I have no doubt He wants to help you get to that place of acceptance as well. When you embrace who God created you to be, you will find confidence and joy. Like the psalmist, you will be able to say, "You created my inmost being; you knit me together in my mother's womb. I praise you because I am fearfully and wonderfully made; your works are wonderful, I know that full well" (Ps. 139:13–14).

Take a moment now, or plan a time in the near future, to stop and write a prayer of commitment to get to know the woman God designed you to be. Study the personality types to see which one or two strike a chord in you. As I mentioned earlier, you might even partner with someone else so you can both uncover your primary and secondary personality type.

Discovering the God-Given Desires of Your Heart

What would you do if neither time nor money was an issue? I love this question because eliminating constraints or excuses often reveals our heart's desire. Once you get beyond the practical, such as paying off your mortgage, or the luxurious, like a month-long vacation in Hawaii, you'll often start thinking about the things that make your heart come alive.

Your heart is the core of who you are, the truest you. The desires of your heart indicate your God-given passion to make a difference somewhere. Often when you see the word *heart* in the Bible, it represents the seat of your emotions or your desires. God's Word tells us to "guard your heart above all else, for it determines the course of your life" (Prov. 4:23 NLT). But many times we hear the opposite. Instead of guarding and listening to our heart, we've been told to silence it and listen to the voice of sacrifice and duty.

What about you? Do you listen to the desires of your heart and live from your God-given passions, or do you serve from a sense of duty and obligation? Many people are unable to answer that question. Some have never thought about it or have stuffed their passions so deeply beneath the busyness of life that they don't have time to find out. Others have neglected their hearts and lived to please people, or suppressed their heart's desires because someone wasn't interested in or criticized their ideas. Even if we do know our heart's desires, for some reason we are really good at making excuses, rationalizing why we haven't stepped out to live our dreams. Author Bruce Bugbee explains that:

> God has put a divine magnet within each of us that is intended to attract us to the people, function or causes where he intends us to minister. This is not an afterthought on God's part. Our passion is built in to us so that we will conform ourselves to His purpose for our lives.[2]

When we don't know what our heart's desires are, we tend to spend our lives fulfilling the desires of others. It's time to ask ourselves the question: "Am I doing what God may be calling others to do, while leaving undone what He is calling me to do?" I want to encourage you to begin to prayerfully pursue your passions, even if it means saying no to what others want you to do—not in a selfish way, but in a way that honors the woman God created you to be.

So how do we discover our heart's desires? Psalm 37:4 says to "take delight in the LORD, and he will give you the desires of your heart." As we find our deepest delight in our personal relationship with God and allow His Word to shape our thinking and plans, the Lord promises to shape our desires as well. There is a connection between our delighting in God and discovering our heart's desires.

Several years ago, I went through a Beth Moore study where she said something that left a lasting impact. I wish I could remember her exact words, but it went something like this: *If you want to know your purpose, pursue the heart of God and you'll have a head-on collision with your calling.*[3] This one sentence helped me stop striving and start seeking instead. And she was so right: the closer I got to Jesus, the more clearly I understood His purpose for my life.

God created your unique heart, and He intends to lead you to the focus of your ministry through your desires and passions. So many needs cry for our attention both inside and outside our homes and churches. We are bombarded with options. It can be overwhelming to choose one thing to invest our time and energy in. But just as a target is designed to narrow the aim of an arrow, God uses the desires of our hearts to narrow the focus of where He wants our lives to make a mark for eternity.

Able or Available?

I opened my front door and saw my friend Janet standing there. Before I could invite her in, she said, "This is the best thank-you note I've ever read. Renee, you have a writing gift and you need to use it." I was confused; it was only a thank-you note. Yet Janet's words replayed in my head all day. I had been asking God for direction and wondered if this was it. Did He want me to encourage more than just one friend with my writing?

His answer came while I was driving home from a women's dinner at my church a few weeks later. I'd taken notes on a napkin, but I wished I had a full outline of the message so I could apply it to my life. Then I got the craziest idea: maybe I could write a study guide to give to other women who want to go deeper too.

Doubt filtered my idea through reality: *Who am I to think I could write something women would want to read?*

I couldn't get the thought out of my head over the next few days, so I told Janet about it and discovered God was answering someone else's prayer too. Janet served on the women's ministry team. She explained how they'd been praying for something to give women after the dinners. Much to my shock, they asked me to write a study guide! I nearly suffocated under a blanket of insecurity, but with Janet's prayers and prodding I wrote it, and over a thousand copies were given away. I wrote another the next year, and then another. I never felt able, but I knew God wanted me to be available.

I haven't always been available. For years I was like the third servant Jesus described in Matthew 25:14–30. Here is my contemporary version of the parable Jesus told: There was a business manager who had three servants. He was going out of town, so he gave each servant an individual project to work on according to his abilities. The first two were entrusted with more responsibility according to their abilities. Perhaps they had more experience or had proven themselves. Both gave their time and talents to serve their boss. He was pleased with them when he returned.

The third servant was given less responsibility, and he neglected his assignment. Maybe he thought, *Oh, this isn't much, why worry about it? My boss will never notice.* Maybe he was jealous. Were the others given more visible responsibilities? Did envy turn to strife toward his boss? Was he apathetic toward his own abilities? Or was he afraid of failing? In any case, the manager was not pleased with him.

I have been guilty of thinking God wasn't fair or didn't love me as much because He didn't give me the talents I admired in others. Unfortunately, I have been jealous when someone was assigned an opportunity I wanted. Just like the third servant, I have sinned by hiding my talents, and I have even felt frustrated with God instead of taking responsibility to be faithful with what I had been given.

These servants had varying abilities, and the master gave them a different number of talents accordingly. However, they were all held accountable to be good stewards of what they had, whether it was large or small. He gave the faithful stewards more and took away what he had entrusted to the unfaithful servant.

Discovering Your Abilities

I wonder how God feels when we are not faithful with abilities He's given us. Honestly, He's our Boss and, in a way, He is on an out-of-town assignment. He has asked each of us to oversee something in His kingdom, according to abilities He's given us. Each ability comes with an assignment. Each assignment comes with the possibility of reward and the potential of regret. It doesn't matter how much or how little God has given to us. What matters is how well we use what we've been given.

Your abilities are the natural talents you are given at birth. Everyone has been given natural abilities, but so many of us let self-doubt shape our excuses: "I don't have any talent. I can't sing. I can't speak in front of people. I can't lead. I don't have anything special to offer." No matter how big or small our talents seem, they are all God-given and can be used for His purposes. I never thought I could write a book. I didn't even think I could write an article. But I did love writing thank-you notes, and that is exactly what God used to lead me to use my writing to help others.

No matter where you are in your spiritual journey, you have something to offer that can make a difference in others' lives.

Perhaps you like to cook; maybe you could use that ability to make meals for shut-ins or new moms. Are you creative with kids' crafts? If so, you could offer to serve at a community outreach center or church. If you have accounting abilities, maybe you could volunteer an hour or two a month to help with administrative needs at a church or assist a neighbor who is having problems balancing her checkbook. God loves to use us, with our unique abilities, to bless those who don't have our same gifts.

It is important to focus on what we have instead of what we don't have. When we are faithful with the little things, God entrusts us with more and we get to share in the joy of fulfilling His purposes. We are stewards responsible for all God has entrusted to us, no matter how significant or insignificant our gifts seem. What step are you going to take to recognize your abilities and be a good steward of them?

Unwrapping Your Spiritual Gifts

Unlike talents and abilities received at natural birth, spiritual gifts are received at spiritual birth. When we accept Jesus as Lord and Savior, God's presence indwells our hearts in the form of the Holy Spirit. Along with His presence comes a "present," more commonly referred to as a *spiritual gift*. It's thoughtfully chosen by our heavenly Father to help us fulfill His plans for us.

Your spiritual gift indicates the way God designed you to serve and complete the body of Christ. We each play a vital role in supporting other parts of the body through love in action. Paul says, "From him the whole body, joined and held together by every supporting ligament, grows and builds itself up in love, as each part does its work" (Eph. 4:16). Without each person knowing and using their spiritual gifts, the body of Christ is incomplete and is hindered from reaching its full potential. Romans 12:5–8 describes seven motivational gifts that I have listed below. Let's take a look at each gift and see if you recognize yourself in one or two of them.

Prophecy

Do you find yourself sharing God's truth, regardless of what anyone thinks? Are you passionate about standing up for something significant? Someone with the gift of prophecy often has spiritual insight into situations and can be a powerful prayer warrior or truth-teller, depending on how God leads.

Teaching

If you have the gift of teaching, you enjoy explaining why things are true. You see the need for biblical knowledge and understanding. Are you interested in research? Do you enjoy digging into details? Someone with this gift loves to learn and share what they discover.

Exhortation

Do you see spiritual potential in individuals and groups? A person with the gift of exhortation loves to encourage the faith of others and help them grow spiritually. These people feel compelled to share God's encouraging words and give practical advice on how to apply God's truth in everyday life.

Mercy

If you have the gift of mercy, you feel compelled to help people reduce pain. Are you concerned more with the person than the reason for their suffering? Many times those with this gift have experienced pain and can therefore empathize with the hurts of others.

Service

Someone with the gift of service often ends up doing what no one else likes to do. If you have the gift of service, you demonstrate love by serving people and enjoy helping others while meeting their needs. You also prefer behind-the-scenes assignments instead of being out front.

Giving

Do you like using your finances to help others? A person with the gift of giving has unique financial insights, often has resources to meet needs, and enjoys sharing material blessings. You see material needs in the church and are sensitive to how money is spent and saved.

Leadership

Do you feel compelled by a strong sense of duty? If you have the gift of leadership, you like to oversee and organize projects and find things for people to do because you see the big picture. You are good at planning for the future while working to keep everyone on track.

Discovering Your Spiritual Gifts

There are three main ways to discover your spiritual gifts. First, the best way to recognize your giftedness is through experience in serving. This may take some trial and error. When my pastor was in the NFL, he became a Christian. He knew God wanted him to serve but he wasn't sure how, so he started in the prayer ministry at his church. Once a month he and his wife also volunteered to rock babies in the nursery. One Sunday, he was asked to share his testimony. He quickly discovered his passion and giftedness for teaching

God's Word. Today he is the lead pastor of one of the fastest growing multiethnic congregations in the United States—but that is not where he started.

Second, you can ask someone who knows you well and has seen you serving. Friends and leaders in ministry are also a good resource to help you find the place in the body of Christ that is best suited for your giftedness.

Third, you can ask yourself this question: "What gives me a sense of joy and fulfillment when I am contributing to ministry or something of spiritual significance?" Remember, your spiritual gifts equip you to fulfill God's purpose by reflecting His design for your life. When we use our divine abilities, God works through us to meet needs in other individuals and the church as a whole.

Life Experiences

Another way God reveals His purpose is through our life experiences. Sometimes they are good experiences, and other times God uses experiences that have been painful or very difficult to get through. We talked in chapter 4 about allowing God to restore our past and redeem our pain for His glory and others' gain. That is what He means in the promise that "in all things God works for the good of those who love him, who have been called according to his purpose" (Rom. 8:28). In her book *Living Life on Purpose*, Lysa TerKeurst describes how God uses our experiences to shape His purpose for our lives:

> Imagine sitting down at a table with two cups of flour, three eggs, a tablespoon of vanilla, one cup of sugar, one teaspoon of baking powder and a few other ingredients. You taste the sugar and it is good, but when you taste the baking powder it is bitter. You continue to taste the ingredients, some tasty

and some downright gross. This is like life. Some of the events in your life are sweet like the sugar, others dry like the flour, and others still that you do not like at all. However, using Jesus' perfect recipe, all of the events of your life will be mixed together and put through some intense heat—and then you will rise. Just as a cake would not be the same if you left out some of the ingredients, so Jesus wants to use all of your life experiences to make you complete and able to be used for His glory.[4]

A confident woman asks God to birth ministry through her burdens by meeting her needs, and then she looks for ways to join Him in meeting the needs of others who are going through something similar. She knows God can use her brokenness to do something beautiful, because the cracks allow His light to shine through and His living water to pour out. Paul describes how this works:

> For God, who said, "Let light shine out of darkness," made his light shine in our hearts to give us the light of the knowledge of God's glory displayed in the face of Christ. But we have this treasure in jars of clay to show that this all-surpassing power is from God and not from us. (2 Cor. 4:6–7)

God also uses positive life experiences to shape our lives for ministry. I have a friend who was a professional wedding planner. She now offers her experience at her church to brides who need assistance but can't afford a professional consultant. Another friend has lots of travel experience. She volunteers her time to plan mission trips. A Christian financial planner whom I know serves on the benevolence committee at his church, helping single moms develop a budget. He also helps determine when they qualify for benevolence assistance.

Has God allowed you to experience something through which you can now see Him working for good in your life or the lives of others? How can you use your unique life experiences to minister to people you meet along the way?

A Beautiful Offering

God designed each of us with the desire to make a difference, and He equipped us to do so through our unique blend of personality, desires, abilities, giftedness, and experiences. These all prepare us for the role we play in the important story He's been writing since the beginning of time.

When my sons were younger, they played for hours on end in our backyard, wielding plastic swords and sticks, pretending to conquer invisible villains. As a little girl, I loved to play dress up. Depending on the day, I was either a princess, a bride, or an ice skater.

Do you remember what you pretended to be as a kid? I wonder if in some way we were all preparing for the important role our hearts longed to play in a story of heroic proportions.

Before the creation of the world, God chose you to be in His story—to be adopted as His daughter, grafted into His family, cast in a leading role, and used for His glorious purpose. Being chosen means you have something special to offer that can make a difference. You are no longer isolated and disconnected. You are wanted, and you belong! A woman with a confident heart chooses to believe that God wants to make an impact through her life, and she looks for ways to let Him.

God made a choice, and now it's your turn. My prayer is that you will choose to become the woman He designed you to be by surrendering your life to Him as a beautiful offering. If you will be true to the person God designed you to be, you will find the life you have always wanted: a life of meaning, purpose, and confidence. Remember, God knows you and loves you just the way you are. The only change He desires is that you become more like Him as you become more like you!

Praying God's Promises

O Lord, You have searched me and You know me. You created my inmost being and knit me together in my mother's womb. I praise You because I am fearfully and wonderfully made; Your works are wonderful and I am one of them. Help me to stop comparing myself with others so I can become the woman You created me to be. I'm one of Your masterpieces, created anew in Christ Jesus so I can do the good things You planned for me long ago. Remind me that You promise to fulfill Your purpose for me and that You will not abandon the works of Your hands.

I surrender my personality, heart's desires, abilities, spiritual gifts, and experiences to Your purposes. I delight myself in You, Lord, trusting You to shape the desires of my heart to match Yours. I want to seek and serve Jesus in all I do, for in Him the whole body, joined and held together by every supporting ligament, grows and builds itself up in love as each part does its work. In Jesus' name I pray, Amen.

See Psalm 139:1, 13–14; Ephesians 2:10; Psalms 138:8; 37:4; 1 Corinthians 12:18; Ephesians 4:16.

Reflection and Discussion Questions

1. "Comparison causes us to compete with each other, but no one wins. God never intended for us to compete with each other; He wants us to complete one another, celebrating and encouraging each other's strengths while discovering who He created us to be" (p. 137). In what areas do you tend to compare yourself with others and

feel like you don't measure up? What did you read in this chapter that can help you break free from the comparison trap?

2. What personality type describes you best? Is there a second personality type that is also strong? Are you content with the personality God gave you? If not, what do you wish was different about yourself?

3. "Just as a target is designed to narrow the aim of an arrow, God uses the desires of our hearts to narrow the focus of where He wants our lives to make a mark for eternity" (p. 144). Do you believe God created you with unique desires and dreams? If you know what they are, list them.

4. What are some of your abilities? If that is hard to answer, list things others have commented that you do well.

5. How did the servant with the least amount of talents perceive His master? Have you ever felt like God didn't give you as much talent or ability as He's given to others? Have you ever buried your abilities because you didn't think they mattered? Has not using your God-given abilities impacted your sense of purpose or your relationship with God? If so, how?

6. Read the following verses and summarize what each has to say about the importance of our spiritual gifts: 1 Corinthians 12:1, 4–7, 11–12, 17–20. These verses describe the importance of understanding and using our spiritual gifts.

7. Has God allowed you to walk through experiences through which you can see Him working for good in your life or in the lives of others? Do you, or will you, use these experiences to minister to others you meet along the way?

I know answering these questions can seem like a lot of information to assimilate. You may be wondering how you will have time to get to know yourself. Remember that getting to know yourself is a process, but also a priority to God. Maybe you can create a half-day mini retreat for yourself. Or if you're in a stage of life where that seems impossible, take an hour each week for a while to go through each section of this chapter in greater detail.

9

When Doubt Whispers "I Can't Stop Worrying"

Rehearsing your troubles results in experiencing them many times, whereas you are meant to go through them only when they actually occur.

Sarah Young[1]

Several years ago, I got to a point where I was absolutely exhausted and ready to resign from just about everything I was doing. I was worried about many things, and it made me weary. I also wondered if anyone noticed or appreciated anything I was doing, which led to feelings of frustration and irritability.

My husband suggested I go away for a weekend to spend some time alone with God. I guess the situation was pretty bad. What man in his right mind sends his wife away for the weekend while he takes care of the kids? When my friend Jen offered me her lake house in the mountains of Tennessee, I jumped at the opportunity.

The first night there, I fell asleep thinking about how I would spend time the next day on the back porch reading, journaling, and praying as I looked out at the lake surrounded by mountains. Unfortunately, the next morning my type-A personality had a hard time relaxing. The things of earth had followed me up the mountain. I was bombarded with thoughts about all I needed to do when I got back home and things I could get done even while I was away.

Distractions and temptations vied for my attention. *If you check your email you'll really be able to relax. And your inbox will be empty when you get home. You know, several people left messages this week and you haven't returned their calls. You could do that now and your list will be checked off. That report is due next week. You could finish it today, and then you could totally focus on God.*

My mind was divided, and my thoughts were scattered in a hundred directions. I decided to flee the temptation of my laptop by going for a walk with my miniature dachshund, which I had brought along to protect me from burglars and bears. I put her on a leash, took my allergy medicine, and headed outside. Breathing in the fresh air, I released my stress by talking to God about all that was on my mind. Soon my heart began to settle, and I felt relaxed.

When I got back to the house about an hour later, I was sneezing and my asthma was bothering me. I couldn't figure out why. I was sure I had taken my allergy medicine. However, when I went back to the bathroom to make sure, I discovered my allergy pill still sitting on the counter. Another bottle with tiny white pills sat next to it. That is when I realized that, in the frenzy of my anxious thoughts, I had accidentally taken my dog's seizure medication instead! Fortunately, she only weighed twelve pounds, so it was just a five milligram dose. After recovering from my disbelief, I took my allergy medication and went out to the porch with my Bible and journal. By then, I couldn't stop laughing. I looked up at the heavens and just had to ask, "Lord, did I look like I was having a seizure?" I'm pretty sure I heard Him chuckle and say, *Yes, child, your brain waves were causing some serious collisions.*

Honestly, I don't think God made me take my dog's medicine, but I do think He may have laughed with me over my mistake. When I finished laughing, though, I thought about how I do sometimes feel like I'm having a mental seizure. My thoughts get divided in many directions and I lose control of my thought processing system, but I didn't realize how serious it was until that day. I was glad I had taken time to slow down and ask God to help me sort out the "things that needed to get done" that were making me come undone.

When Our Concerns Consume Us

With your many roles, responsibilities, and relationships, do you ever get overwhelmed? Do your worries ever make you weary?

Even when we're physically present in today's tasks, our minds tend to live in tomorrow's troubles, don't they? Before we know it, our concerns can consume us. While I sat on the porch talking to God and journaling, He reminded me of a woman in the Bible who also got consumed by her concerns. Like me, you may be familiar with her story. If so, I hope you won't just glance over it, but will join me in looking for some new truths in an old passage. Let's visit the house of Mary and Martha together and see what we can learn:

> As Jesus and his disciples were on their way, he came to a village where a woman named Martha opened her home to him. She had a sister called Mary, who sat at the Lord's feet listening to what he said. But Martha was distracted by all the preparations that had to be made. She came to him and asked, "Lord, don't you care that my sister has left me to do the work by myself? Tell her to help me!"
>
> "Martha, Martha," the Lord answered, "you are worried and upset about many things, but few things are needed—or indeed only one. Mary has chosen what is better, and it will not be taken away from her." (Luke 10:38–42)

I used to defend Martha, thinking, *Well, nobody was helping her; it's no wonder she was upset. Somebody had to be in the kitchen. Who was going to cook and wash the dishes?* Then a pastor told me there were likely servants there whom Martha could have delegated to. That's when I knew she probably had control issues. Few of us will admit it, but I think we all have a little control freak inside us that freaks out when we get overly worried and weary.

Have you ever noticed that when circumstances in your life feel out of control, you'll start trying extra hard to control things like your kids, your husband, or the clutter around your house? One night I started freaking out a little because my fifteen-year-old had not put his clean clothes away. They remained stacked on his dresser for a whole week, and he'd thrown dirty clothes on top of them. When I asked him to clean his room, he ended up putting the folded clean clothes back in the hamper with his dirty clothes.

It had been one of those days where life felt out of control and nothing was going right. I let my frustrations spew out on my son. My words were harsh and my reaction excessive. What I said wasn't wrong, but how I said it was. Here I was trying to control something—but now it was controlling me. Then I couldn't sleep that night because I felt bad for being so critical with my son, which only added to my worries and made me more weary. Has that vicious cycle ever happened to you?

Many Things

Jesus told Martha that she was "worried and upset about many things." I wonder if she didn't even realize it. There are times when I don't realize I'm worried. My mind is wired to think a lot, so I get used to the constant flurry of motion in my brain. Worry will slowly start to creep in, and before I know it there's a stirring in my heart, my neck gets tense, my mind won't shift gears, and little concerns kick into full-blown worries.

Too often, instead of talking to Jesus, I think a lot of times we just start talking to ourselves in our heads until our accumulation of concerns become worries. Yet Jesus invites us to come and talk to Him. He promises a resting place for our restless hearts. He says, "Come to me, all you who are weary and burdened, and I will give you rest" (Matt. 11:28).

When I surveyed women on my website, asking them to describe the "many things" they worry about, their responses included:

- "How I am going to get it all done. I lie in bed with all of these thoughts running through my head about everything that needs to be done. I feel like I'm always playing catch up."

- "I worry about finances. I worry about what people think of me. I worry about my kids and their choices."
- "I worry about anything I can't control, so basically I worry about everything. Money, raising kids, the safety of my loved ones."
- "I'm a single mom with two kids. I worry about finances, losing my job in today's economy, and raising them without a godly male influence."
- "I worry that I will never overcome my sins and find victory in my life."
- "I'm a natural worrier. I think my biggest worries are personal concerns. I seem to be able to trust God with everyone else's prayer requests, and know and believe that he's working on their behalf, but when it comes to my worries they seem to multiply and become greater than reality."

Over and over women mentioned finances, marriage, children, and the salvation of loved ones. What are the many things that make you worried and weary? Take a few minutes now to write them down on a piece of paper.

But If I Don't Worry, Who Will?

I used to think that if I wasn't worried about something, then God wouldn't be either. Have you ever thought that if you stopped thinking about a problem it would move off God's radar screen? Perhaps we see ourselves as God's assistants, reminding Him of things on His to-do list each day. I think Martha may have had that mind-set. But her worries didn't change anything except the condition of her heart and the atmosphere of her home, and the change wasn't for the better.

In his book *Come Thirsty*, Max Lucado shares his thoughts on worry:

> When was the last time you solved a problem by worrying about it? Imagine someone saying, "I got behind in my bills, so I resolved to worry my way out of debt. And, you know, it worked! A few sleepless nights, a day of puking and hand wringing. I yelled at my kids and took some pills, and—glory to worry—money appeared on my desk."
>
> It doesn't happen! Worry changes nothing. You don't add one day to your life or one bit of life to your day by worrying. Your anxiety earns you heartburn, nothing more.
>
> Regarding the things about which we fret:
>
> - 40 percent never happen
> - 30 percent are in regard to unchangeable deeds of the past
> - 12 percent focus on the opinions of others that cannot be controlled
> - 10 percent center on personal health, which only worsens when we worry about it
> - 8 percent concern real problems that we can influence.[2]

If only 8 percent of our concerns are problems we can influence, why do we spend so much time worrying? I think it's because we have a hard time trusting God completely. Also, we have an enemy who wants to convince us that we are the only one who can change things. He wants us to doubt God's sovereignty and question His ability to care for us. The enemy talks us into believing that we need to worry about the people and problems in our lives because God's got bigger things to worry about. He's got world peace and the health-care crisis to worry about. He's busy, you know. The war in the Middle East is much more important than the war we have with our worries, right?

Worry Robs Us

Jesus warns us in John chapter 10 that our enemy is a thief. One of his most effective robbery attempts is through a string of worrisome thoughts. We need to recognize his schemes and realize the effects they have on us. An acronym that helps me remember how damaging worry can be is: **W**orry **O**nly **R**obs **R**est from **Y**ou.

- Worry robs us physically, leaving us exhausted.
- Worry robs us emotionally, leaving us anxious.
- Worry robs us mentally, leaving us scattered.
- Worry robs us spiritually, leaving us depleted.

When I feel exhausted, anxious, scattered, and depleted, I can easily start to doubt myself. I lack energy to handle my day-to-day events and just want to run away. I get overwhelmed with a sense of uncertainty.

- I doubt I can manage my life.
- I doubt I can hear God clearly.
- I doubt I can do all God has called me to do.

Worry also robs us of our confidence that God notices and cares about the details of our lives. Remember how Martha questioned whether Jesus cared that her sister left her in the kitchen all by herself to do all that work? Do you ever wonder if God notices and cares about things that are concerning you—how you will get everything done, how you will pay bills, how your children will handle you going back to work and not spending as much time with them?

God notices and He cares. Just listen to the words He had King David use to describe how well He knows you. Why not read them out loud:

> O LORD, you have examined my heart
> and know everything about me.
> You know when I sit down or stand up.
> You know my thoughts even when I'm far away.
> You see me when I travel
> and when I rest at home.
> You know everything I do.
> You know what I am going to say
> even before I say it, LORD.
> You go before me and follow me.
> You place your hand of blessing on my head. (Ps.
> 139:1–5 NLT)

Worry also robs us of peace in our relationships with others. Not only was Martha questioning God, she was mad at her sister. That happens to me too. Overwhelmed by all of my responsibilities and efforts, I can get frustrated with people closest to me. I have said to my husband, "Don't you care? Don't you notice all I'm doing? Why don't you help me?"

That is exactly what the enemy wants. Jesus warned that the enemy "comes only to steal and kill and destroy" (John 10:10). He wants to rob us of rest and destroy our relationships with God and others. He is a thief and he will take more than our peace if we let him.

Living in the Middle of Impossible

As we learn from Martha's story and relate it to our own, we realize she was at a dinner party. Her concerns were simple compared to the harder things we may be going through. Just like Jesus helped Martha see what her worries were doing to her, He wants to do the same for us, no matter what our situation may be.

Our family has been through the hardest year of our lives: a good friend and mother of three young children died from breast cancer, we switched our sons' school, we adopted a baby from Ethiopia, our twelve-year-old got swine flu the week before we left for Africa, and we all got very sick while we were there. At the same time, our ten-month-old adopted daughter, Aster, had pneumonia and wanted nothing to do with us. After traveling for thirty hours to arrive home with our new family of five, we finally started adjusting to life with a baby and tween/teen boys.

A month later my mom was hospitalized for eight days with blood clots in her lungs, a kidney infection, and a kidney stone that required surgery. Afterward she moved in with us. My dad had to have open-heart surgery a month later, and I had an abnormal mammogram that led to a biopsy. All this happened in six months. Once I got my feet on the ground again, I started writing a book while also traveling to speaking events, all of which had been contracted before we knew any of this was going to happen. There is so much more I could share, but I just don't think I can describe another thing. Basically, I was living in the middle of impossible.

I thought I was handling it well, although I had a few meltdowns. Eventually, I realized it was affecting me more than I had recognized. I couldn't concentrate on anything, my memory was disappearing, and I vacillated between feeling numb and restless.

I remember telling my husband it felt like fifteen people were in my head all talking at the same time. This was very out of character for me. I decided to go online and take an ADD assessment, where I scored very high and convinced myself that was the problem. I didn't have time to go to the doctor, so I decided to change my diet and do the best I could to manage my life.

The Day I Lost It

"Where is the stroller?" my mom asked as I changed Aster's diaper.

"The stroller? I don't know. I thought you had it."

"No, it was not in the van Friday when I needed it."

I had left Friday morning to speak at a women's event in Illinois, so I assumed my husband, JJ, had used it, but he said he'd been looking for it, too. I was baffled. I had it while I was shopping with Aster the Thursday before I left town. I guessed that, after I put Aster in her car seat, I had forgotten to go back and put the stroller in our van. I was parked in front of a building, so I had backed out and didn't even see my stroller. I hadn't even noticed it was gone.

I wish I could say it was the only thing I'd lost. That same week I had lunch with a friend. She said the blessing and then got up to get something. When she came back I asked her to pray before we started eating. It had only been three minutes, and I had already completely forgotten we had prayed. Then I went to the dry cleaner to pick up a few things. When I woke up the next morning, I realized I had paid for the cleaning but walked out without my plastic sheath–covered garments. I felt like I was losing my mind.

That is when I decided to call my doctor and set up an appointment to get medicine for adult ADD. She got me in the next day and listened as I described our past year. I told her my diagnosis, and then she started asking questions: "Are you sad? Have you been having any trouble sleeping? Do you have any chest pressure? How about headaches or other pains?"

I cried when she asked about feeling sad. I was very sad that I was losing my memory and my brain power. I had a book to write and a baby to take care of and I really needed my mind back. The floodgates broke when I responded "yes" to the rest of her questions. What came next sent me into a state of shock.

My doctor looked at me and said, "Renee, people don't get ADD in their forties. I believe you have developed stress-induced anxiety, and it's gone on so long you now have anxiety-induced depression."

Tears streamed down my face as I tried to convince her I was not depressed. *I went through depression twenty years ago. I know what it felt like. This is not the same. I don't want to commit suicide, although I would be really happy if Jesus came back soon. I don't stay in bed all day, although I am exhausted all the time.*

She told me this was different and asked me to try a new medication to see if it would help. She tried to make me feel better by telling me about the several other women my age she saw each week who were going through the same thing, but I still didn't want to hear what she was saying.

However, I had asked friends to pray God would show my doctor what was wrong. I knew she was a Christian, and I sensed that He wanted me to trust the Holy Spirit in her. She loved me with her words, and I could tell she sincerely wanted to help me. She asked if she could pray for me, and as she laid her hands on my shoulders, I felt God's peace and assurance.

The Strength of My Heart

I went downhill for two more weeks before I started feeling better. Not only did I feel overwhelmed, sad, and anxious, I felt lost inside the maze of my thoughts. I wondered why God was allowing this to happen after all that I had already been through. My footing seemed like it was slipping out from underneath me. The writer of Psalm 73 penned words that echoed my feelings: "But as for me, my feet had almost slipped; I had nearly lost my foothold" (v. 2).

Like the psalmist, I lost perspective for a little while when I looked at others who were doing well despite their own crazy lives. I wondered how and why I had slipped into this pit. I knew that only God's power in me and me putting my trust fully in Him could get my feet back on solid ground. Like the writer of Psalm 73, I had to shift my focus to the only place I could find the security and strength I needed: my relationship with God.

> Yet I am always with you;
>   you hold me by my right hand.
> You guide me with your counsel,
>   and afterward you will take me into glory.
> Whom have I in heaven but you?
>   And earth has nothing I desire besides you.
> My flesh and my heart may fail,
>   but God is the strength of my heart
>   and my portion forever. (vv. 23–26)

I love how he replaced his confusion and defeat with the refuge of God's strength and comfort.

Can you think of a time when it felt like your footing had slipped out from underneath you? Have you gone through seasons of stress that have led to anxiety and depression? I share my story so that you will know you are not alone. Worry can have serious side effects. Sometimes when our bodies endure ongoing seasons of prolonged stress, our body chemistry gets out of balance. Some people can get back on track by making lifestyle changes, while others may need medication.

God made us. He is the Great Physician. I believe He gave doctors wisdom, and if we are under their care and seeking

Christian counsel, we can trust God to help us through them too.

Out of Balance

For me, it was more than a chemical imbalance. My heart was also out of balance. I had gone through so many emotional changes and intense spiritual storms. There was so much pressure on me from every side that I didn't know how to slow down and process it with God as deeply as I needed to. Although I was praying, journaling, and reading my Bible, my time with Him was more like a drive-thru devotion than the five-course meals my soul needed. When I spent time with God, I did most of the talking. I needed to balance it out with more time spent listening to God and allowing His perspective to shape mine.

Mary sat at Jesus' feet *listening* to what He said, but Martha didn't. Instead of going to Jesus with a listening heart, Martha went to Jesus with a "listing" heart. She was listing her questions and then her instructions. I lived with a never-ending list of things I needed to do and problems I needed God to solve. Unfortunately, on too many occasions my list became the focus of my time with God.

The Bible tells us to come to God with all of our concerns, even when there is a long list of them. The difference is we give Him our lists and our hearts, saying, "Lord, this is what's on my mind. This is what I'm worried about," but instead of telling Him what to do, we stop and ask, "Lord, what is on Your heart? What are Your thoughts toward me? What are Your thoughts about this situation?" And then we listen. When we find the important balance between talking and listening to God, we position ourselves to hear what He has to say.

Are God's Promises Big Enough for My Problems?

In Philippians 4, Paul gives us a prescription for God's peace in the midst of our problems. First, he reminds us the Lord is near. Then he instructs us:

> Don't worry about anything; instead, pray about everything. Tell God what you need and thank him for all he has done. Then you will experience God's *peace*, which exceeds anything we can understand. His *peace* will guard your hearts and minds as you live in Christ Jesus. (vv. 6–7 NLT, emphasis mine)

Now that is a big promise! When my worries make me weary, I need God to guard my heart and mind with His peace as I tuck myself into Jesus and live in the security of His sovereignty. Let's break down the steps Paul gives us to get God's peace:

- **Stop worrying**—press the pause button on my consuming concerns.
- **Start praying**—open my mouth and tell God what I need.
- **Keep thanking God**—remind my heart of God's goodness by thanking Him for what He's done.

That sounds doable, but why is it so hard? I think it's because the thief whispers the opposite: *Do not be calm about anything; instead worry about everything. Tell God what He should do. Then take control if He doesn't listen. And the concerns that consume your thoughts will devour your peace as you wring your hands, allowing anxiety and doubt to rob you of joy!* Unfortunately, we listen to him, don't we?

In the NIV translation, verse 7 says, "The peace of God, which *transcends all understanding*, will guard your hearts and your minds in Christ Jesus" (emphasis mine). Wouldn't it be great if it said God's peace would transcend my *need to understand*? I think I could more easily accept what God is doing if He'd help me understand why He's doing it. But God doesn't promise understanding; He promises peace in the midst of not understanding. His nearness can be our good, and finding a refuge of peace in Him can be our goal (Ps. 73:28).

Not only does God want to give us peace that surpasses our understanding; He wants to surpass our need to understand with promises that are bigger than our problems. Psalm 55:22 tells us, "Turn your burdens over to the LORD, and he will take care of you" (GW). Now let's pull out our lists of "many things" I asked you to write down earlier and turn these burdens over to Jesus. Then read the promises below out loud until you believe them, and let God replace your worries with His peace.

- "You make known to me the path of life; you will fill me with joy in your presence" (Ps. 16:11).
- "The LORD is my shepherd, I shall not want" (Ps. 23:1 NASB).
- "Show me your ways, LORD, teach me your paths. Guide me in your truth and teach me, for you are God my Savior, and my hope is in you all day long" (Ps. 25:4–5).
- "Whoever dwells in the shelter of the Most High will rest in the shadow of the Almighty. I will say of the LORD, 'He is my refuge and my fortress, my God, in whom I trust'" (Ps. 91:1–2).
- "Though I walk in the midst of trouble, you preserve my life. You stretch out your hand against the anger of my foes; with your right hand you save me" (Ps. 138:7).

- "The LORD will work out his plans for my life—for your faithful love, O LORD, endures forever. Don't abandon me, for you made me" (Ps. 138:8 NLT).

Sometimes I Have to Boss My Heart Around

I caught my heart heading to the pit of discouragement for spring break during my year of "impossible." It was supposed to go to the beach with me and my family, but it was not cooperating. I have a feeling Martha would understand. She probably had an idea of what the dinner party was going to be like and how much she would enjoy it. But then nothing went the way she planned, and her heart headed to the pit.

Did you notice how Martha started bossing Jesus around? When she was mad about Mary not being in the kitchen, she went to Jesus and said, "Tell her to help me!" I admit I have a tendency to be a little more bossy when I'm stressed and worried too. However, I've learned that instead of bossing others around, I need to boss my heart around. I don't have to go to the pit of discouragement and pull others in with me. That is never part of God's plans—nor mine.

King David was really good at telling his heart and soul what to do. In Psalm 103 he said: "Praise the LORD, my soul; all my inmost being, praise his holy name" (v. 1). During spring break, I decided to follow his example in the midst of my troubles. Although a close friend had found out she might have ovarian cancer, our air conditioning broke, our taxes were much more than we expected, and I couldn't meet my book deadline *again*, I told my soul to praise the Lord.

Now this wasn't a superficial "say your bedtime prayers" talk to my soul. No, this was a deep down, preach it to my inmost being, GOD IS GOOD no matter what sermon. I bossed my heart with God's truth and pulled her away from the pit by telling her to "forget not all his benefits" (Ps. 103:2). Then I walked my heart down memory lane, reminding her of the One who:

> Forgives all [my] sins and heals all [my] diseases,
> redeems [my] life from the pit
> and crowns [me] with love and compassion,
> who satisfies [my] desires with good things
> so that [my] youth is renewed like the eagle's. (Ps. 103:3–5)

No matter what the answer was to my friend's diagnosis, how much our broken air conditioner was going to cost, how much we owed on taxes, or how delayed my book release was going to be, my soul needed to praise the Lord. Instead of worrying, I knew God wanted me to worship Him by remembering and focusing on all He had done, was doing, and would do in my life as I trusted Him.

Discerning between Good Things and God's Things

Sometimes we don't even know what to tell our hearts to do. Oftentimes we expect more of ourselves than God expects from us. Martha's "many things" looked like good things: she wanted to serve Jesus and His friends. But her good things weren't all God's things for her that day. Sometimes we can get into the habit of serving God more than we are seeking Him, and we end up distracted and depleted. Has that ever happened to you?

My husband and I had prayed about all of our commitments and made major cutbacks before adopting Aster and signing a book contract. However, in hindsight we see that as unexpected crises came, one right after the other, we should have made even more cutbacks.

We tend to expect too much of ourselves and think we can do more than is realistic, but we also learn the most from our biggest mistakes. Believe me, I learned a big lesson that I pray I'll never forget. God taught me a lot about limits and setting healthy boundaries. Although I was doing good things, not all of them were God's things for me during that season. Martha was more focused on serving Jesus than seeking Jesus. But Jesus told her there was only one thing she needed. Mary had *chosen* that one thing, a better thing. It's not that Martha's choice was bad. It's that Mary chose what could not be taken away: time spent with Jesus.

Spending Time with Jesus

I used to think being a godly woman meant getting up early to spend time with Jesus praying and reading my Bible. The only problem is that I don't process thoughts or words early in the morning. I would beat myself up with guilt for being distracted and groggy. One day God interrupted my thoughts with this thought: *Renee, I made you. I know you are not a morning person. I know you like variety. I created you, so work with Me. Spend time with Me in the beginning of your day, as soon as you can, but don't feel like it has to be the same time in the same place again and again.*

From that point on, my time with God has been more adventurous and enjoyable. I do aim for the morning. If I start my day listening and talking with Him, when He whispers something to my spirit during the day I can discern His voice more clearly. It's like I have cleaned out the clutter in my mind and prepared my heart to hear His voice.

Often women will ask me how I find time to spend with Jesus, and what I do during that time. First, I don't find time, I choose the time. Spending time with God is a high priority, and when my life is really busy, I actually schedule it in my planner. Here are a few other ideas that might be helpful.

Plan a D.A.T.E.

Determine A Time Every day to spend with Jesus. Just like with any other relationship you value, you have to be intentional and plan time together. You won't just find yourself sitting on the couch reading your Bible. Be sure to plan a date.

Set Realistic Expectations

If you are just starting out, begin with ten or fifteen minutes and build from there. The more time you spend with God, the more you'll want to spend with Him, eventually. Plan a shorter morning devotion for each day and more extensive study of God's Word at times during the week when you have fewer interruptions.

Create a Setting for Two

I have a chair in my bedroom where I can get away from distractions to meet with Jesus. I keep my Bible, journal, a pen, a small notepad, and my Bible study or devotion book in a basket next to my "Jesus chair." If I'm hurrying out the door and didn't spend time with Jesus that morning, I picture Him waiting for me to come back. I know Jesus is always with me and lives in me, but it helps me to picture Him wanting to spend time with me.

Read God's Word

Everything you need to know about God is in His Word. If you've never read the Bible, I encourage you to start in the Gospel of John, and get to know Jesus. Then read through the New Testament.

Journal What God Shows You

We've talked about taking our thoughts captive and listening to God's truth over Satan's lies, but we won't know what is true if we haven't spent time with God and recorded Scriptures He's shown us. Be sure to take time to write down what He's showing you, or I can promise you won't remember it later.

Use Scripture for Conversation Starters

I love to use Scripture to start my conversations with God. As we have seen, when we pray God's Word for ourselves or insert others' names, we can be sure we are praying God's will.

Reflect on God's Faithfulness

In my journal, I also write down thoughts and prayers. Periodically I will read through my journal to reflect on what God has done. Many times I won't even remember what I had prayed. If I don't journal, I don't remember all that God has done. When I find myself in a struggle, I can cling to God's faithfulness by reading my journal and reflecting back on how He's come through again and again.

Some days I sit with Jesus and do all these things. Other days I go running in the morning and listen to my *GoBible Traveler*.[3] Then I'll talk to Him and listen to His Spirit speaking to mine while I am walking back home. Sometimes I bring my spiral index cards with verses written on them and pray them out loud. I also love to look up at the sky and focus on my Creator, thanking Him for the gift of beauty in nature.

Before your worries make you weary or your concerns get consuming, I pray that you will recognize what is happening and ask Jesus to give you a resting place for your restless heart. When things you want to control start to control you, ask God to help you let go and trust that He is in control. I hope you will schedule dates for the next thirty days to spend time with Jesus. Find a place where you enjoy being with Him.

When you feel worried, talk to Jesus instead of talking to yourself. Instead of bossing others around, boss your heart around by reminding it to remember who God is—and how good He is at being God. Remember that more than simply serving Him, God wants you to seek Him. He wants you to sit with Him so He can give you His perspective and fill your heart with confidence in His presence each day.

Praying God's Promises

Search me, O God, and know my heart; try me and know my anxious thoughts. See if there is any hurtful way in me, and lead me in the everlasting way. When concerns consume me, remind me that You are with me, holding me by my right hand and guiding me with Your counsel. Though my flesh and my heart may fail, You are the strength of my heart and my portion forever. Help me turn my burdens over to You, knowing that You will take care of me.

Because You are my shepherd, I shall not be in want. You promise that when I dwell in the shelter of the Most High, I can rest in the shadow of the Almighty. You are my refuge and fortress, my God in whom I trust. Though I walk in the midst of trouble, You preserve my life; You stretch out Your hand against the anger of my foes, and with Your right hand You save me. Thank You for making known to me the path of life and filling me with joy and peace in Your presence. In Jesus' name, Amen.

See Psalms 139:23–24; 73:23–26; 55:22; 23:1; 91:1–2; 138:7; 16:11.

Reflection and Discussion Questions

1. How often do you feel exhausted, anxious, scattered, or depleted?

2. When you get overwhelmed, do concerns ever consume you? If so, what does that look like in your head and heart?

3. Do you ever catch yourself wondering if God notices everything you are doing? Do you ever doubt you can do all He has called you to do? Are there some things in your life He may not expect or want you to be doing?

4. If Jesus came to your house this past week to spend time with you, would you have been able to walk away from unfinished laundry, dishes, or emails if He wanted to talk with you? Imagine hearing Him say, "You are worried and upset about many things." What were some of your many things?

5. What will you do for the next thirty days to make sure you have a date (Determine A Time Every day) to be with Jesus? Is there someone you can ask to help or to hold you accountable to spending time with God, so you can listen more closely for His plans, rest in His promises, and experience His peace?

6. Which of God's promises in this chapter will you cling to so that you don't lose your footing and slip into a pit of discouragement?

7. How can you transition from going to God with a list to going to Him with a listening heart? What are some practical things that can help you relax and listen to God in the midst of your busy life (walking, journaling, listening to music, taking a bubble bath, etc.)?

10

When Doubt Whispers "I Can't Follow God Consistently"

> When I come to the Lord after I've blown it, I come with only one appeal: His mercy. I've no other defense. I can't escape my biggest problem: me! So I leave the courtroom of my own defense. Because of what Jesus has done, God looks on me with mercy. It's my only appeal, it's the source of my hope, it's my life.
>
> Paul David Tripp

Have you ever felt like God is ready to give up on you because you don't follow Him consistently? Do you sometimes fear that God's tolerance for your shortcoming is limited and that you are one step away from being disqualified from His grace?

Several years ago I blew it and felt sure that God was ready to give up on me. I was preparing to speak at my home church's women's retreat. It was an honor, but I was nervous to follow in the footsteps of some amazing speakers who had gone before me. Four weeks before the retreat, I needed to turn in my outlines, but I hadn't finished one of my messages. JJ offered to hang out with our boys on Saturday, and my mom offered her home to me to study and spend time alone preparing. I told her I needed several hours of quiet and didn't want to impose. She insisted she'd be gone all day running errands and didn't mind if I used her place.

JJ and I sat down and made a schedule that morning before I left. I wanted to make sure he stopped mowing the lawn in time to take a shower and get the kids ready to meet me at my mom's house by 5:15 p.m., since he and I needed to leave no later than 5:30 p.m. for a surprise party. The birthday girl, my friend Debbie, would arrive around 6:00 p.m. and we needed to get there before she did. Once our plans were firm, I went to my mom's house.

Reading my Bible, praying, and listening for God's direction for hours were like being in a spiritual oasis. I was studying about Jesus being the bread of life. Then I cross-referenced the Old Testament where God provided manna in the desert for the Israelites, which was their "bread of life." I thought about spiritual deserts we go through and how God wants His Word to be the manna in our deserts and tough times. I loved the message God was giving to me.

Desert Storm

As I watched the hours go by, I asked God to stretch out my time with Him. Studying in the quiet of my mom's house helped me concentrate and get into a "zone" where God was revealing new insights faster than I could type. I love that place, but it takes time to get there. Once I am in the zone, I don't want to come out of it because I'm afraid I won't be able to get back in. That is when I start thinking, *Don't anybody talk to me. Don't make noises and knock me out of my zone.* About that time my mom decided to come home—early. She was quiet for about thirty seconds, but then she started bringing in cement pavers and dropping them on the floor. Then she carried in groceries and plopped them down in the kitchen where I was studying. Next came the opening and closing of doors, followed by the sound of her going up and down the stairs. Within minutes, I was out of the zone. Panic set in. I didn't have my message complete and my time was up.

I decided to stop working. When I stood up to close my laptop, I accidentally hit my water bottle, tipping it over and spilling it into my keyboard. Frustrated and ready to scream, I reached for towels to soak up the water from my computer and the floor. Not only had I come out of my zone, a desert storm was rising up within me. *What if my computer is ruined? What if I lose my message notes? What if I totally blow it at this retreat?*

My mom was upstairs, so she didn't know what was going on. I decided to take a shower and get ready, hoping it would also help me calm down. About an hour later, as I was finishing up, my mom noticed her tablecloth was wet. I had forgotten to take it off. When she lifted it, there was a big white cloud on her antique oak table. Being understandably upset, she started ranting to me, "I can't believe you did this. Don't you know when you spill water on an oak table you're supposed to take the tablecloth off?"

And You Call Yourself a Christian?

Like a scolded child, my defenses went up. I blurted out an apology and tried to explain what had happened. Then I noticed it was 5:30 and JJ still wasn't here. We were supposed to be leaving, so I called his cell phone but got no answer. Anxiety spilled like acid in my heart: *What if JJ had an accident? What if we get to the party late and Debbie sees us in the parking lot and we ruin the whole surprise? What if this stain doesn't come out of Mom's table?*

Since the police hadn't called, I determined JJ was just running late. By 5:40 p.m. I decided to leave without him since he could just meet me there. As I was pulling out of the driveway, he drove up. Much to my surprise he didn't hurry out of his car, and he had this "I knew you would be mad" look on his face. My youngest son got out of the car, walked up to me quietly, and said, "Daddy told us you would be mad." I decided to leave before I said something I would regret.

As I pulled past his car, JJ asked, "Are you not going to wait for me?" My window was rolled up, so I only saw his lips moving. I rolled the window down so he'd ask again: "Are you not going to wait for me?"

Being all mature, I said, "No. Because you're acting like an [beep]." (You know, the biblical word for mule.)

Right then my eight-year-old son walked out of my mom's house and said, "Mommy! You just called Daddy an [beep]."

"Well, he's acting like one," I explained.

And wouldn't you know, just as I blurted that my mom walked out and heard the whole thing. She said she couldn't believe I said that to my child, and then she added, "And you call yourself a Christian speaker!?"

What Was I Thinking?

I apologized, rolled my window up, waited for JJ to get in the car, and left for the party. We smiled at everyone else but only spoke a few words to each other all evening. On the way home we mumbled apologies.

The next morning, I was overwhelmed with shame and guilt. I kept thinking about my mom's words. How could I call myself a Christian speaker? I had no business teaching a message I couldn't even live. I started beating myself up with statements like, *I'm not cut out for this. I'm not good enough. I'm not godly enough. What was God thinking when He called me to this? What was I thinking?*

How could I move from a place of spiritual depth to such a place of spiritual depravity? I had been praying, studying, and reading my Bible. Why didn't I apply what God taught me just that day? Looking back, I can see that I had needed to stop and ask God for manna in my desert. I needed His peace and perspective in the midst of my storm, but I didn't even think to ask Him in the heat of the moment. Instead I had allowed my emotions to run wild within me.

When I walked into church that Sunday morning, I scanned the auditorium looking for MaryAnn, my women's ministry director, friend, and mentor. I had decided to tell her I was stepping down. I walked up with tears in my eyes and said, "I've made a huge mistake. I'm so sorry. I never should have said yes to speak at this retreat. You're going to have to find somebody else."

After I explained what happened, she looked at me and said, "Renee, if you don't need this message as much as the women attending, then you are not qualified to teach it. But because you need it as much as we do, you are qualified. You have been appointed and you are anointed to do this."

Letting God's Grace Cover My Guilt

I had never experienced such a demonstration of God's grace. Later that day, I thanked God for His unmerited favor and forgiveness. I also asked for His perspective. He covered me with His grace by reminding me of men and women in Scripture whom He used greatly—despite their downfalls. He also reminded me that JJ and I had prayed for weeks before I said yes. I also had dates written in my Bible next to verses He'd given me as confirmation. That day, I learned to live in the promise that I can "approach God's throne of grace with confidence, so that [I] may receive mercy and find grace to help [me] in [my] time of need" (Heb. 4:16).

Although I was ready to give up on me, God wasn't. Although I was deeply disappointed in myself and felt like such a disappointment to God, He took what felt like destruction and used it for reconstruction in my walk with Him. I learned that when I confess my sins and receive God's forgiveness, my heart is set free from guilt-induced doubt and I can find grace-induced confidence (1 John 1:9). I'm not saying there weren't consequences. It took time and a lot of apologizing to restore things with my mom and my family. Still to this day they tease me about cursing at Daddy.

A month later, I spoke at the retreat, and I sensed God wanted me to share that story of my falling so short of His glory. Did I fear people would judge me? Yes. But like Paul, I discovered that God's grace is sufficient because His power is made perfect in my weakness. Although telling on myself is humbling, God has convinced me to "boast all the more gladly about my weaknesses, so that Christ's power may rest on me" (2 Cor. 12:9). Women shared how much that story impacted them because they blow it just like I do, and I had helped them see God's grace on the other side.

I want you to know we all blow it, but God offers grace to cover our guilt. Satan wants us to think we're the only ones who mess up, but it happens to all of us, every day. When I asked women if they ever doubt they can follow God consistently, I was flooded with "yes" responses.

Whether we allow others' negative attitudes to affect us, break our promises to God, fight with our husband, don't spend enough time (or any time) praying and reading the Bible, or stop going to church, we feel that way. Or when we yell at our kids, overeat, let the stress and strain of everyday life bump God to the bottom of our priority list, hold grudges, act prideful, or do anything we think or know a Christian shouldn't do—we doubt our ability to follow God consistently. It's one of our biggest struggles.

God's Riches at Christ's Expense

I used to feel so far from God, like I had to work my way back to Him after periods of inconsistency in my time with Him, seasons of unbelief or self-sufficiency, or other sins. I was also convinced God had lost His patience with me. Then I'd try harder and eventually fail again. Finally, I'd get defeated and wonder, "What's the use in trying?"

But now I know it's not about trying harder. It's about turning sooner. It's about confessing sin and turning back to God's gift of grace. Grace is God's "undeserved favor." We don't have to earn it, and we cannot lose it when we act undeserving. An acronym for grace is God's Riches At Christ's Expense. Yes, grace cost a lot, but Jesus already paid for it. Remember, it is "by grace [we] have been saved, through faith—and this not from [ourselves], it is the gift of God" (Eph. 2:8).

Some people ask if grace is a license to sin. A confident woman knows that it's not. Instead, she realizes grace is the security of knowing God's love is guaranteed for her because she trusts in Christ. Really understanding His sacrificial gift accomplishes the opposite of granting a license to sin. When we grasp what Jesus did for us, we want to return the gift of His life by offering ours to Him, even if our offering isn't perfect or even perfectly consistent.

God's Patience in the Process

Have you ever talked to someone who was going through a struggle, and instead of feeling sorry for them, you felt better at first because it let you know you weren't the only one who struggled with that same thing? Then you felt bad for feeling good about their struggle. That is how I felt when I read the rest of Gideon's story about overcoming his doubts and fears: let's just say it took him awhile. I love that, because overcoming doubt has been such an ongoing process with me too.

Walking with God consistently is about trusting Him entirely and following Him fully in our thoughts and actions. What I love about Gideon's story is how very patient God was with him over the time it took for Gideon to trust God completely. As we will see, Gideon's faith was inconsistent but God's patience was absolutely constant. Let's go back and look at what was happening before God came to Gideon:

> Again the Israelites did evil in the eyes of the LORD, and for seven years he gave them into the hands of the Midianites. Because the power of Midian was so oppressive, the Israelites prepared shelters for themselves in mountain clefts, caves and strongholds. Whenever the Israelites planted their crops, the Midianites, Amalekites and other eastern peoples invaded the country . . . and did not spare a living thing for Israel. . . . Midian so impoverished the Israelites that they cried out to the LORD for help.
>
> When the Israelites cried to the LORD because of Midian, he sent them a prophet, who said, "This is what the LORD, the God of Israel, says: I brought you up out of Egypt, out of the land of slavery. I rescued you from the hand of the

Egyptians. And I delivered you from the hand of all your oppressors; I drove them out before you and gave you their land. I said to you, 'I am the LORD your God; do not worship the gods of the Amorites, in whose land you live.' But you have not listened to me." (Judg. 6:1–10)

God had done everything to provide for the Israelites. He commanded them to worship Him alone, but they didn't listen. Instead they worshiped their enemies' gods, which made them vulnerable to their enemies' destruction. Eventually they cried out to the Lord. Because God's love is patient, He came to their rescue and raised up the least likely leader to guide them to victory.

The angel of the LORD came and sat down . . . where . . . Gideon was threshing wheat in a winepress to keep it from the Midianites. When the angel of the LORD appeared to Gideon, he said, "The LORD is with you, mighty warrior."

"Pardon me, my lord," Gideon replied, "but if the LORD is with us, why has all this happened to us? Where are all his wonders that our ancestors told us about when they said, 'Did not the LORD bring us up out of Egypt?' But now the LORD has abandoned us and given us into the hand of Midian." (Judg. 6:11–13)

Why Does It Have to Be So Hard?

I remember asking God the same thing: *Why has all this happened? Why does it have to be so hard?* Why couldn't I just prepare my message without interruptions, arguments, cursing at my husband in front of my child, and spilling water in my computer?

Sometimes life is hard because we live in a fallen world or we're experiencing a spiritual attack. Other times life is hard

A Confident Heart

because we're not listening to God or following what He has shown us, as was the case for both the Israelites and me. When life is hard, though, we are more likely to ask for God's help. I know it's true for me and for others I've talked to. Tough times often precipitate movement toward God and help us depend on Him more than on ourselves. That happened to me this past year. Life was too much for me to handle, but I depended on God like never before.

Do you ever ask God why life has to be so hard? Why certain things happen? Like Gideon, do you feel abandoned by God during disappointments or troubled times? At one point I felt that way, when so many hard things were happening at once. I think we all do at times, but our feelings don't change God's promise that He will never leave us nor forsake us (Deut. 31:8).

So what do we do? God tells us to "Trust in the LORD with all your heart and lean not on your own understanding; in all your ways submit to him, and he will make your paths straight" (Prov. 3:5–6). Let's see how God responded to Gideon's questions: "The LORD turned to him and said, 'Go in the strength you have and save Israel out of Midian's hand. Am I not sending you?'" (Judg. 6:14).

Notice how God didn't answer Gideon's "why" question. Instead God told him what role He was calling Gideon to play in what He was about to do next. Perhaps that is because God had already explained through the prophet that their hard circumstances were the consequences of their sin. Sometimes when we ask God why, He shows us how our sin played a role in whatever is happening. Other times it's much harder to process, because the trouble isn't caused by anything we or anyone else has done.

My friend and author Lysa TerKeurst has experienced tragedy in her life that left her with many "why" questions and not many answers. She learned that "asking why is perfectly normal. Asking why isn't unspiritual. However, if asking this question pushes us farther from God rather than drawing us closer to Him, it's the wrong question."[1]

We will see that God used Gideon's "why" question to draw Gideon closer to Himself, because His answer shifted Gideon's focus from hard things that had happened in his past to what God was about to do in his future. God told Gideon he was going to be part of making things better by saving Israel from the Midianites. Sometimes God answers our prayers by calling us to be part of the solution to our problems. Instead of changing our circumstances, often God uses our circumstances to bring us closer to Him, make us more like Him, and help us find our confidence in Him.

It's Hard to Trust Someone You Don't Know

Up to this point, Gideon knew about God, but he didn't know God personally. He had heard others talk about God and share stories of what He had done for them in the past. That is why he asked, "Where are all [God's] wonders that our ancestors told us about when they said, 'Did not the LORD bring us up out of Egypt?' But now the LORD has abandoned us and given us into the hand of Midian" (Judg. 6:13).

Gideon's perception of God included feelings of reverence but also abandonment. Maybe he didn't realize the Israelites' decision to disobey the Lord and worship other gods had been what got them into such a mess. Maybe he had been praying for a long time that God would help them, and he'd given up.

Because God chose to come to Gideon instead of someone else, I believe Gideon must have been seeking God and desired to follow Him. Second Chronicles 16:9 tells us that "The eyes of the LORD search the whole earth in order to strengthen those whose hearts are fully committed to him" (NLT). We will see the Lord strengthening Gideon's heart over time. Although God told Gideon He was sending him, and that He would go with him and give him strength to defeat the Midianites, Gideon didn't yet trust God. It's hard to trust someone you don't know.

> Gideon replied, "If now I have found favor in your eyes, give me a sign that it is really you talking to me. Please do not go away until I come back and bring my offering and set it before you."
> And the LORD said, "I will wait until you return." (Judg. 6:17–18)

When Gideon brought his offering, the angel of the Lord touched it with the tip of his staff and fire flared from the rock, consuming it. Then Gideon realized it was in fact the angel of the Lord and exclaimed, "Alas, Sovereign LORD! I have seen the angel of the LORD face to face!" (v. 22).

Up to this point, Gideon had called Him "Lord." Now he used the word "Sovereign" to describe his Lord because he had experienced God's sovereignty. Another layer of confidence was built when Gideon witnessed God's power—but that's not all. Gideon must have looked terrified, because immediately, "the LORD said to him, 'Peace! Do not be afraid. You are not going to die'" (v. 23).

I love what Gideon did next: "Gideon built an altar to the LORD there and called it The LORD is Peace" (v. 24). God had revealed His character by demonstrating His power and by giving Gideon peace to help him overcome his doubts and fears. Gideon not only knew about God, now he was getting to know Him personally. He would learn that it's much easier to trust someone you know—someone you have experienced life with in a personal way.

Lord, I Want to Know You

Close relationships are built over time when we share life together, moving from a place of hearing about someone to seeing them live out who they really are. My friend LeAnn is someone I have gotten to know over time and come to love as I have experienced her love for me.

At first, I'd only heard wonderful things about LeAnn from other people. Then we started working in the same office, and I observed things about her that matched what others said, but there was more. There were things that I only discovered by being with her, like her unique sense of humor and her way of making others feel special.

As our friendship deepened and we shared more of our lives with each other, I came to trust her. I can call her when I am worried or discouraged, and she will calm me down. She knows just what to say. She is someone I know I can depend on—but I only know that because I have needed to depend on her, and she has been dependable.

Getting to know God happens in the same way. We may have heard or think we know many things about Him, but we won't really know Him until we spend time with Him, talking, listening, and observing who He is. Our depth of knowing God comes when we depend on Him and discover that He is dependable. We learn to trust His heart by interacting with Him and experiencing His character in personal ways, like Gideon did.

I have a list of several of God's names that I carry in my purse and in my journal. My friend Kimberly sent them to me when I was going through a tough time because she knew I needed to be reminded of who my God is. It helps me to say these names out loud and to thank God for being each of these things for me; to say, Lord, thank You that You are:

- *Emmanuel*: My God with Me (Matt. 1:22–23)
- *El-Channun*: The Gracious God (Jon. 4:2)
- *El Hanne'eman*: The Faithful God (Deut. 7:9)
- *El Roi*: The God Who Sees Me (Gen. 16:13–14)
- *El ha-Gibbor*: The Mighty God, God the Hero (Isa. 9:6)
- *El Shaddai*: The All-Sufficient God (Gen. 17:1–2)
- *El Sali*: God of My Strength (Ps. 42:9)
- *El Olam*: The Everlasting God (Gen. 21:32–33)
- *El Elyon*: The Most High God (Dan. 4:34)
- *Elohim*: God, My Mighty Creator (Gen. 1:1)
- *Jehovah Jireh*: The Lord Who Will Provide for Me (Gen. 22:13–14)
- *Jehovah Rapha*: The Lord Who Heals Me (Exod. 15:26)
- *Jehovah Nissi*: The Lord My Banner (Exod. 17:15–16)
- *Jehovah Shalom*: The Lord My Peace (Judg. 6:24)
- *Yahweh Tsuri*: The Lord My Rock (Ps. 144:1)
- *Jehovah Rohi*: The Lord My Shepherd (Ps. 23:1)
- *Jehovah Shammah*: The Lord Is There for Me (Ezek. 48:35)
- *Abba*: My Father (Ps. 68:5–6)

God's names are a promise of who He is. We learn to trust Him as we come to know Him in the way He is described in the Bible, based on His character. We will not know God as *Jehovah Rapha*, our Healer, until we experience and recognize His healing in our lives, whether spiritually, emotionally, mentally, or physically. We cannot know Him as *Jehovah Jireh*, our Provider, if we are not in need. We will not know Him as *Jehovah Nissi*, our Banner, unless we need Him for victory.

As we seek to follow God more consistently, let's start praying, "Lord, I want to know You for who You really are. I desire to trust and follow You more and more each day." We will grow in our consistency and confidence as we live in the promise: "Those who know your name trust you, O LORD, because you have never deserted those who seek your help" (Ps. 9:10 GW).

What Am I Afraid Of?

After proving His power and providing His peace, God told Gideon to tear down his father's altar to the false god Baal, get one of his father's bulls, and sacrifice it on a proper altar that he would build for the Lord. Gideon did as God told him, but "because he was afraid of his family and the townspeople, he did it at night rather than in the daytime" (Judg. 6:27). God's mighty warrior was still afraid. Instead of walking in faith, he was living in fear.

Many times it's our fears that keep us from following God consistently. We're afraid of people's criticism, judgment, and rejection. We're afraid to say no because someone might get mad. Many times, we're more afraid of disappointing people than we are of disappointing God. We're afraid to trust God with our money, time, marriage, or kids, so we try to manage our own lives. We don't stand up for what we believe because we're afraid people will be offended by our faith. Many women have told me they don't read the Bible because they're afraid they won't understand it. Some are afraid to pray because they don't know what to say.

Doubt is often fueled by fear. Fear can be powerful and paralyzing to our faith. I know because I have been its victim. As I shared in chapter 1, fear-infused doubt kept me from enjoying carousel rides as a child, waterskiing as a teen, and trust as a new bride—but that is not all. I had accepted my fear like it was a handicap I was born with. I let fear permeate every area of my life.

During my early years of marriage, I was afraid to sleep at night whenever my husband traveled for work. I knew I needed to trust God, but I didn't. In addition to praying, reading my Bible, and taping verses to my bedside table and mirror, I slept with my phone, the neighborhood directory, and my Bible.

One night I also put toys on the stairs to trip any burglars, put my children in my room to sleep with me, and put my dresser in front of my bedroom door. I thought I was controlling my circumstances, but instead fear had taken control of me. When I still couldn't sleep, I opened my Bible and read these words:

> Do not fear, for I have redeemed you; I have summoned you by name; you are mine. When you pass through the waters, I will be with you; and when you pass through the rivers, they will not sweep over you. *When you walk through the fire, you will not be burned; the flames will not set you ablaze.* (Isa. 43:1–2, emphasis mine)

That night God helped me see that my fears were like flames and my efforts to protect myself were like gasoline. Every time I did something, it was like pouring fuel on the fire. My fear was consuming me. God reminded me that He had not given me a spirit of fear but a spirit of power and love and a sound mind (2 Tim. 1:7).

I realized the only way I would overcome my fears was by walking through them. I would have to put away my props and go to bed trusting God and not myself, knowing that even if my fears came true He would be with me. That night I put everything away and walked through the flames of my fear. I did what God was calling me to do, and I slept better than I had in weeks.

Jesus said, "If you hold to my teaching . . . then you will know the truth, and the truth will set you free" (John 8:31–32).

Fear lost its power when I actively held on to the promise He's given me.

If we want to be free from fear so that we can walk in faith, we have to hold on to what God is teaching us, replacing our ways with His. We will only overcome our fears by walking through them, holding God's hand and trusting His heart to lead, protect, and preserve us.

Two Steps Forward, One Step Back

When the Midianites found out Gideon had destroyed Baal's altar, they gathered their forces of 135,000 men and prepared for battle. Then the Spirit of the Lord came upon Gideon. He took his first step of faith by blowing a trumpet, summoning allies to follow him, and sending messengers throughout the region, calling his people to arms. But something happened, and Gideon got scared again.

> Gideon said to God, "If you will save Israel by my hand as you have promised—look, I will place a wool fleece on the threshing floor. If there is dew only on the fleece and all the ground is dry, then I will know that you will save Israel by my hand, as you said." And that is what happened. Gideon rose early the next day; he squeezed the fleece and wrung out the dew—a bowlful of water.
>
> Then Gideon said to God, "Do not be angry with me. Let me make just one more request. Allow me one more test with the fleece, but this time make the fleece dry and let the ground be covered with dew." That night God did so. Only the fleece was dry; all the ground was covered with dew. (Judg. 6:36–40)

Can you see why I love this story? It's such a picture of our back-and-forth faith. Gideon needed more assurance and God gave it to him. Again, we see amazing evidence of

God's grace and patience. He's still there with us, even when we take two steps forward and one step back. He knows that our faith is not about our performance but our dependence on Him. Gideon may have been afraid, but what mattered most is that he sought God to give him confidence.

From Wimp to Warrior

God didn't want the Israelites taking credit for the victory He would give them, so He told Gideon:

> "You have too many men. I cannot deliver Midian into their hands, or Israel would boast against me, 'My own strength has saved me.' Now announce to the army, 'Anyone who trembles with fear may turn back and leave Mount Gilead.'" So twenty-two thousand men left, while ten thousand remained. (7:2–3)

Aren't you proud of Gideon for not leaving with them? Sometimes staying is a step of faith.

God told Gideon there were still too many men and instructed him to take them to a stream to see how they drank water. Only three hundred drank by cupping their hands and bringing water to their mouths, which was important because they could keep their eyes up and still see their enemies. With these three hundred men, God told Gideon He would save him and give the Midianites into his hands. Gideon sent the rest of the men home (vv. 4–8).

> During that night the LORD said to Gideon, "Get up, go down against the camp, because I am going to give it into your hands. If you are afraid to attack, go down to the camp with your servant Purah and listen to what they are saying. Afterward, you will be encouraged to attack the camp." (vv. 9–11)

God knew what Gideon needed. Did Gideon take advantage of God's "if you are afraid" clause? You bet he did. He and Purah went down to the enemy's camp, where they heard a man talking about his dream and how the Midianites were growing afraid of Gideon and his army (vv. 13–14).

> When Gideon heard the dream and its interpretation, he bowed down and worshiped. He returned to the camp of Israel and called out, "Get up! The LORD has given the Midianite camp into your hands. . . . Watch me," he told them. "Follow my lead. When I get to the edge of the camp, do exactly as I do." (vv. 15, 17)

What a difference! I can almost hear the confidence in Gideon's voice. This was a man who had lived in fear, but now he was a courageous leader. By seeking to know and choosing to trust God, a wimp became a warrior.

Gideon's three hundred men followed his lead, doing everything he said to do. While they stood in their positions around the camp, every one of the thousands of Midianites ran, crying out as they fled. God caused them to turn on each other with their swords. The odds may have been against Gideon, but God was for him! With God's help, Gideon and his army defeated their enemies.

Gideon learned to follow God more consistently by depending on God's strength instead of his own. He shifted his focus from doubting himself to believing his God. More than just helping him conquer the Midianites, God also helped Gideon conquer his personal enemies of doubt and fear. And He wants to do the same things in our lives. Oftentimes God will use our doubts to build our confidence by calling us to face our fears and do something we would never choose to do on our own. But when we depend on Him, we experience victory we never thought possible.

In Dependence

There will be times when we will not follow God consistently and we'll start to doubt the strength of our faith. Those times usually come when we are thinking and operating independently from God. Oftentimes our behavior is due to fear, but other times it could be unbelief, worry, stress, or simply our desire to manage our own lives. Yet we were created to live "in dependence" on God.

Transitioning from living independently to living in dependence on God takes time. It's a lifelong journey. Sometimes it can feel like Gideon's battle, but usually that is because God has something amazing for us on the other side, and our enemy doesn't want us to get there. Like Gideon, we need to stay close to God and keep asking Him to show us Himself.

We also need to remember that "our struggle is not against flesh and blood, but against the rulers, against the authorities, against the powers of this dark world and against the spiritual forces of evil in the heavenly realms" (Eph. 6:12). Satan will do all he can to keep us from becoming confident women in Christ. As I shared before, we don't need to be afraid, but we do need to be aware and prepared for his strategies.

When we blow it and Satan tries to tell us we can't follow God consistently, we don't have to listen to him. We can turn away from the shadow of doubt and stand in the light of God's truth. The truth is no one can follow God perfectly, without any inconsistencies. But we can follow God more consistently each day as we come to know Him and choose to trust Him with our lives.

When your walk with God wavers, when you feel like you're taking two steps forward and one step back, review Gideon's story. Remember God's patience in the process, and let His grace cover your guilt. Reflect back on Gideon's transformation from wimp to warrior, and ask God to give you the confidence to live a transformed life as well. Remember, God is not looking for a woman who is perfect. He is looking for a woman who wants to walk with Jesus and find her confidence through her daily dependence on Him.

Praying God's Promises

Lord, thank You that I can approach Your throne of grace with confidence and receive mercy and find grace to help me in my time of need. Because of Your mercy and forgiveness, my guilt-induced doubt is replaced by grace-induced confidence. Help me trust You with all my heart and not lean on my own understanding, acknowledging You in all my ways so You can make my path straight. Those who know Your name trust You, Lord, because You have never deserted those who seek Your help.

I want to know You as Emmanuel—My God with Me; El Hanne'eman—My Faithful God; El Roi—The God Who Sees Me; El ha-Gibbor—God My Hero; El Shaddai—My All-Sufficient God; El Sali—God of My Strength; El Elyon— The Most High God; Jehovah Jireh—My Provider; Jehovah Rapha—My Healer; Jehovah Nissi—My Banner; Jehovah Shalom—My Peace; Yahweh Tsuri—My Rock; Jehovah Shammah—The Lord Is There for Me; and Abba—My Father. In Jesus' name I pray, Amen.

See Hebrews 4:16; 1 John 1:9; Proverbs 3:5–6; Psalm 9:10.

Reflection and Discussion Questions

1. Have you ever blown it and felt like God was ready to give up on you? Do you sometimes doubt God's grace and patience with you? If so, describe what happens

and how doubt perpetuates more doubt and distance from God.

2. What mistakes or struggles make you feel like you can't follow God consistently? With each one, picture yourself walking to the cross and asking Jesus to speak words of grace over your guilt. He invites you to "approach the throne of grace with confidence, so that [you] may receive mercy and find grace to help [you] in [your] time of need" (Heb. 4:16).

3. Sometimes life's hardships make it hard to follow God consistently. Do you ever ask God why life has to be so hard? What did you learn from Gideon's story? How can his experiences about asking why and trusting God's promises help you as you take the next step He may have for you?

4. Have you ever prayed for God to change your circumstances and instead He changed you through your circumstances? If so, describe what happened and how it helped you grow closer to Him.

5. What did you learn about the importance of knowing God intimately and experiencing aspects of His character to build your trust in Him?

6. What names and characteristics of God do you need to live "in dependence" on in your life right now? Ask God to help you, and look for promises that assure you of His faithfulness. Journal how your confidence grows as you depend on Him more each day this week.

7. Describe an area of your life, or role you have, where you feel like a wimp and you want God to make you a warrior. Through dependence on Him, what would it look like for you to be "more than a conqueror through Him who loves you" (Rom. 8:37) in that area or role?

11

The Woman I Want to Be

Your past has not come full circle to its complete redemption until you allow Christ to not only defuse it, but also to use it.

Beth Moore[1]

They will be called oaks of righteousness, a planting of the LORD for the display of his splendor.

Isaiah 61:3

I used to dream about the woman I wanted to be. She was fun, encouraging, trustworthy, loving, and real. I also wanted her to be confident, but that seemed like something you were either born with or not. As you know, I wasn't naturally gifted with that trait. Over the past few years, though, I've discovered it is my birthright to be secure as a child of God. Through these pages I have shared with you the journey of discovering the inheritance of my Father's promises and claiming them as my own. By living like they are true, I am becoming the woman I want to be, a woman with a confident heart.

My deepest desire is that you are too! I want you to know I have prayed for you and will continue to do so. I have claimed God's promises over your life, and I believe He is already completing the work He's begun in you. I guess you should also know that I went ahead and promised Jesus, on our behalf, that:

> [We will] not throw away [our] confidence . . . [we will] persevere so that when [we] have done the will of God, [we] will receive what he has promised . . . [because] we do not belong to those who shrink back and are destroyed, but to those who have faith and are saved. (Heb. 10:35–36, 39)

As we end this part of our journey together, I want you to know that living in the power of God's promises isn't a one-time thing. I return to every truth I have shared with you, again and again. I pray you will keep this book as a resource so you have easy access to God's perspective and His promises that remind you how much He wants you to have a confident heart. I also pray you will pass a copy on to someone else so that God's confidence will spread into the hearts of all His children.

In chapter 12, "Living in the Security of God's Promises," I have compiled many of the verses we have talked about—and more—so that you can copy them, pray them, and carry them with you in your heart and in your purse! I hope you will memorize them, pray them out loud, claim them as your own, and keep relying on Jesus to live like they are true.

A Planting of the Lord

As you become confident in Christ, you will become a display of God's splendor. He will use your transformed life to show off His glory. There is nothing more fulfilling than asking God to reveal Himself to you and then letting Him reveal Himself through you. I hope you will take what you have in Christ and give it away. I pray that you will become a catalyst for other women to learn to live in the power of God's promises because they have seen it happen in you.

Living and giving away what you have will happen as you surrender your life to Jesus. It's a glorious adventure—but it may not always look the way you think it will. It may even require some replanting of things that have grown comfortable, but I promise you can trust God with all your heart. He wants to bless you!

One Saturday afternoon, I decided to tackle some long overdue yard work. As I headed out to our shed, I noticed a rosebush the previous homeowner had planted. It was in full bloom, displaying its splendor through gorgeous pink blossoms across the center of our split rail fence. *How did that happen?* I wondered.

I had never done anything to care for it. Although I had seen a green bottle of rose fertilizer in our shed, I had not used it before. I decided this would be a good day to start. So, I bent down on my knees and pulled the weeds away from the bush's base so the plant food could sink into the soil. That is when I noticed the root ball had four sections. I wondered if I should leave the sections all together, or divide and place them at different posts on the fence.

If I planted them at separate posts, their vines would eventually connect and create a blanket of pink draped across the whole fence. With that image in mind, I knelt before the blossoming beauty and pressed my hands into the dirt to find the right places to separate the root ball.

For the Display of His Splendor

At that moment, I sensed God whisper to my heart that the rosebush was a picture of what He was doing in my life. I had just found out MaryAnn, my close friend, women's ministry director, and mentor, was moving. Her husband's pastoral position at our church had been unexpectedly eliminated. I was devastated. When I got the news, all I could think was, *How am I going to make it without her?*

This was a woman who had believed in me much more than I ever believed in myself. She had invested in me and encouraged me. She had prayed for me and stood beside me. She had helped me overcome many fears and doubts, which helped me have the courage to follow God's call in my life. I didn't know if I'd have the confidence to keep taking courageous steps of faith without her.

Besides that, we had one of the most thriving women's ministries in the country. I had hopes of serving beside her, and other women I loved, until we died. We had all been carefully planted in our giftedness, nurtured and encouraged through prayer, equipped through training, and fertilized by opportunities to serve. We had become a display of God's splendor. What was God doing with MaryAnn's departure?

I wondered if we, like my rosebush, had reached the fullness of His splendor in our current soil. I couldn't bear the thought, but I had a feeling there would be more pruning to come. I sensed Him telling me we were ready to be divided into separate plants so that His glory would be more fully displayed. He would plant each of us uniquely and individually in new places of ministry, inside and outside our church.

A Place of Surrender

I doubted what God was doing at the time. Yet, as I imagined God's splendor being more fully displayed, my heart settled into a place of surrender. It wasn't my plan, but if it was for

His glory, wasn't that what I wanted? Would I trust Jesus to bring something good from it?

That day I knelt on holy ground in front of my rosebush and surrendered my dreams and plans. Even if it meant letting go of what I loved so deeply, it would be worth it if others would see Him more fully in my life and eventually in my ministry.

Jesus' life and death display God's promise to turn our losses into a legacy when we surrender our lives to Him. I didn't think I could make it, but now I see how God used that season of replanting to overcome my doubts. He wanted me to depend solely on Him for my confidence. He used that season to draw me into a place of sweet surrender.

It was worth it—because Jesus is worth it. However, there are times when I still get worn out and want to give up because surrender is hard. Sometimes I fall on my knees, or cry in my heart, *God, I can't do this!* He always reminds me, *I don't want you doing this. Empty your heart of all of you, so you can be filled with all of Me.* Then He leads my heart back to Jesus and reminds me of everything He did for me, surrendering through His death so that I could truly live.

Remember how I shared that this past year I had to have a biopsy? It was a really big concern, because my mother and three cousins have had breast cancer. I went through a time of fear and sadness, but finally I surrendered again. Here is what I wrote in my journal:

December 30, 2009
    Lord, what will I do if I have cancer? How will I respond? What changes will that bring? What treatment will I need? My mind wonders if the results are negative, will I trust You? Will I believe You answered my prayer to reveal any cancer and not let them miss anything?

My heart is in a wobbly place, teetering between hope and fear, confidence and doubt. Please infuse my soul with faith to believe and trust Your ways and Your timing. Jesus, I don't want cancer. I don't want to settle for believing that it's my destiny just because it's in my history. The past doesn't define my future; You do. You are the One who knows the plans You have for me, plans to prosper me and not to harm me, plans to give me a future and a hope. Oh, Jesus. This is my hope: that You are good, that You are loving, that You are able and willing to heal and restore, to redeem and remake.

I stand at the foot of the cross, knowing I must lay my body down before You. I want to be willing to become a vessel that You can use through whatever circumstances You allow. Like so many other times before, it's in my suffering I see and share in Your glory. And isn't that what I was made for? Like Jesus, I want to be a reflection of Your glory, a representation of who You are.

Father, make me a willing vessel to surrender and rest in You no matter what. I pray that You will keep my heart in perfect peace, because my mind is steadfast as I trust in You. No matter what tomorrow brings, may You find me faithfully available to lay it all down before You as a sacrificial offering of praise.

It's 4:12 p.m. and as I was writing this prayer, my cell phone rang. It was the radiologist calling a day early to tell me my biopsy came back benign. Oh Jesus, thank YOU!!!

In the Shadow of the Cross

Perhaps you have noticed that the desire to "walk away" is one of my default emotions when life and ministry are more than I can handle. I wish it weren't, but it is. One day, I was in a really hard place, and I told God I was done. I didn't have the strength to keep going. I remember Him impressing my heart with a thought I never had before: *Renee, you will only experience My resurrection power if you are willing to die to yourself and rely on Me. You must stay in the shadow of the cross.*

I felt led to actually lie down on the floor and picture the shadow of His cross over me. I could almost feel the resurrection power that raised Jesus from the dead rise up in me and give me strength to keep going. In the shadow of the cross, I was reminded that day that:

> I have been crucified with Christ and I no longer live, but Christ lives in me. The life I now live in the body, I live by faith in the Son of God, who loved me and gave himself for me. (Gal. 2:20)

Jesus did not die on the cross just to get us out of hell and into heaven. He died on the cross to get Himself out of heaven and into us! It's what we were made for. That is why we long for glory. The truth is, we were created to reveal glory—just not our own. God created us in His image to reveal His glory by giving visibility to His invisible character within us. Christ *in us* is the hope of glory (Col. 1:27).

Oh, how the world needs to see, feel, and experience Jesus! God wants to give us confidence in Christ that others can see, so they will want Him for themselves. It's time that we, God's girls, let Jesus have His way in our lives. Let's make a promise that every time doubt casts its shadow over us, we will run back to Jesus, turn toward the light, and stand in the shadow of the cross where everything changes. In the shadow of the cross:

- When you feel inadequate, God says: **You are CHOSEN.** "'You are my witnesses,' declares the LORD, 'and my servant whom I have chosen, so that you may know and believe me and understand that I am he'" (Isa. 43:10).

- When you feel afraid, God says: **You are REDEEMED.**
  "Do not fear, for I have redeemed you; I have summoned you by name; you are mine" (Isa. 43:1).
- When you feel unloved, God says: **You are LOVED.**
  "You are precious and honored in my sight, and . . . I love you" (Isa. 43:4).
- When you feel forgotten, God says: **You are REMEMBERED.**
  "See, I have engraved you on the palms of my hands" (Isa. 49:16).
- When you feel insecure, God says: **You are SECURE.**
  "Let the beloved of the LORD rest secure in him, for he shields him all day long, and the one the LORD loves rests between his shoulders" (Deut. 33:12).
- When you feel unable or unstable, God says: **You are ABLE.**
  "The Sovereign LORD is my strength; he makes my feet like the feet of a deer, he enables me to tread on the heights" (Hab. 3:19).
- When you feel worthless, God says: **You are CALLED.**
  "You are a chosen [woman], a royal [priest], a holy [daughter], God's special possession, that you may declare the praises of him who called you out of the darkness into his wonderful light" (1 Pet. 2:9).

Is God Enough?

As we live in the power of God's promises, we will still have struggles. Don't ever let doubt convince you that you are not a strong Christian or that you will never have a confident heart because you still struggle. As we become the women we want to be, and more importantly the women God created and called us to be, we will still go through times when we have questions and doubts. Sometimes we may even ask, *Is God enough?*

I have shared how God has become my "enough," but I want you to hear from someone else who has asked that question in the face of many doubts, losses, and fears. My friend, speaker, and author Melissa Taylor shared these words in a devotion she wrote for Proverbs 31 Ministries:

> Is God enough? It's a question that my life circumstances force me to keep going back to. What I've concluded is that not only is God enough, but He has to be enough. I've also concluded that it takes effort on my part to keep myself aware of this.
>
> As a young child, I didn't realize my need for God, but I did realize that I had a need that was not fulfilled. I was sexually abused when I was seven years old. My dad left our family when I was eleven. Both circumstances left me devastated, and I didn't understand how God could bring healing at that time. I spent many years trying to heal myself and make myself feel better. Nothing worked.
>
> As I grew older and began to move from being a Christian who simply believed to a Christian who was actively involved with Jesus, my life began to change. Because I was having conversations with Him directly and reading His Word consistently, my life was challenged. I learned that when the hard knocks came, and they would, I needed to ask myself one question in order to move on: "Is God enough?"
>
> - When a friend betrays me, is God enough?
> - When I need to forgive someone for something that seems unforgivable, is God enough?
> - When my child is having issues that are out of my control, is God enough?
> - When my marriage is on the brink of destruction, is God enough?

- When I am not forgiven by another person, is God enough?
- When my mother is dying of cancer, is God enough?
- When others don't recognize my value, is God enough?
- When I am struggling professionally, is God enough?
- When someone I love uses words to hurt me, is God enough?
- When I am in debt and don't know how I'll pay my bills, is God enough?
- When I am reminded of something I did in the past, is God enough?
- When the world is in turmoil, is God enough?
- When my health is declining, is God enough?
- When I am let down and disappointed in my life, is God enough?

Just last night, I sat in my room crying. Here I was again, asking, "Is God enough?" I opened a box full of personalized Bible verses that someone very special gave to me. I began reading them out loud to myself. Verse by verse, I began combating the thoughts that were paralyzing me with self-doubt. What I discovered is the conclusion I always come to when I ask myself "Is God enough?" Yes, He is.

I could lose everything in life. There's not anything I have here on earth that is guaranteed. If I lost it all, though, I'd be okay because no one can take away my identity in Christ. Whether I live in a mansion on a hill or a shack in the swamp, I have my Jesus. Whether the world is for me or against me, I have my Jesus. When I am knocked down, I get on my knees and there I find my Jesus. His Word is planted deep in my heart and I believe it all.

When life becomes more than you think you can handle, don't quit. And certainly don't believe the lies you may be entertaining in your head. Instead, ask yourself, "Is God enough for me?" The answer could change everything.[2]

As you can see, Melissa's faith has been tested by many trials, but she has learned to trust and believe God's promises. She is a beautiful display of His splendor. Not only has God given Melissa hope by proving He is enough for her, God is also using Melissa to share that same hope with other women. Through her writing, her words of encouragement, and her prayers, Melissa ministers to women around the world every day. I know of a few who have chosen not to take their lives because Melissa shared how God could be enough for them too.

The Power of Prayer

God will use our lives to touch others, but our most important ministry will be within our homes. Our trust in God's promises will preach the most powerful sermon when it's lived out in everyday life. I encourage you to ask God to reveal doubts and insecurities He's healing in you that your kids, your husband, or your mom may also struggle with. Then share promises with them that you are holding on to, and pray for their hearts to grow confident in Christ too.

God is also using my friend Melissa to show her children that He is enough through the power of prayer. When Melissa's son Dylan was nine years old, he had to have lab work done involving needles and drawing blood. Dylan had been diagnosed with generalized anxiety disorder, which doesn't go well with needles. He practically hyperventilated upon just hearing what would be done to him. His breathing became short, and he went into panic mode just listening to the doctor explain the details.

Melissa had been working with Dylan on speaking up for what he needed, so he decided this was a good time to put that into practice. "Can we please wait one week to do this lab work?" Dylan asked. The doctor asked, "Why?" To which he replied, "I'd like to get my mom's friends to pray for me." The doctor agreed that was a great idea.

When they got home, Dylan told Melissa, "Mom, if you will get all of your praying friends to please pray for me to be brave and unafraid, I know it will work." So of course, she did. Not only did her friends pray for Dylan, they emailed letters to him sharing their exact prayers and their words of encouragement. Dylan believed them and he trusted in the power of prayer. He believed God heard them, and a week later he went to the lab.

Melissa could tell Dylan was nervous, but he kept saying, "God is with me and will get me through this. I will trust the Lord with all my heart." At that moment he needed to decide, "Is God enough to get me through this?" His answer was, "Yes." The nurse stuck the needle in his arm and five vials of blood were drawn. When it was over, Dylan exclaimed, "That's it? It's over? The prayers worked!"[3]

The Power of Encouraging Words

The disciple John tells us that the power of God's love helps us overcome doubt and fear when we activate it by practicing love with others:

> My dear children, let's not just talk about love; let's practice real love. This is the only way we'll know we're living truly, living in God's reality. It's also the way to shut down debilitating self-criticism, even when there is something to it. For God is greater than our worried hearts and knows more about us than we do ourselves.
>
> And friends, once that's taken care of and we're no longer accusing or condemning ourselves, we're bold and free before God! We're able to stretch our hands out and receive

what we asked for because we're doing what he said, doing what pleases him. . . . As we keep his commands, we live deeply and surely in him, and he lives in us. (1 John 3:18–24 Message)

One day God gave me courage I'd never known before. I was in a situation where I had to choose whether or not I would show His love by helping someone overcome their fear of heights, which is also a huge fear of mine. I can't stand balconies, and when I drive across a bridge, you'll find me hugging the rail along the inside lane. Some friends tried to help me conquer my fear by inviting our family to an indoor rock climbing center.

My heart stopped as we entered the doors and I scanned the highest peak, which stood at twenty-five feet. The instructors assured me that a web of ropes and harnesses would hold me tight. Before I could say "no, thank you," I was strapped in and signing an injury waiver.

Toward the end of the day, our friends John and Laura encouraged their eight-year-old son Steven to climb the highest peak, promising tokens and ice cream if he did it. Steven was a little afraid of heights, too, but he loved a dare. The promise of reward, mixed with the challenge and faith of his father, evoked courage in him.

I watched with admiration as Steven started the climb with confidence. He made it to ten feet, then fifteen, then twenty. But as he inched past the next face of the wall, he saw how far he still had to go. In fear, he looked down and claimed he couldn't do it. Then he cried out for his daddy's help.

By this time, Steven's dad was holding their very tired three-year-old and his mom was feeding their hungry baby girl. I don't know where my brave husband was, but I quickly realized I was the only one standing there who could do something. Suddenly courage and strength surged through my body, and I called out, "Don't give up, buddy. You can do it. I'll help you!"

In record time, I reached the twenty-foot marker, crossed over the peak, and came up beside Steven to encourage him, reminding him of how far he'd come. I told him he could do it with God's strength and that it would be worth it if he'd persevere. With my words and my confidence in him, I helped Steven turn his thoughts toward a higher goal, an inner peak, a reward much greater than ice cream and game tokens: the reward of getting to a place he had stopped believing he could reach.

Funny how I stopped thinking about my fears when I was focused on helping someone else overcome his. I realized that the same promises I had claimed for Steven were true for me too. I could also do it with God's strength, and I did!

Each day we have the same opportunity. Like God did with Gideon, and like He does with us, we can come alongside others in some of life's hardest challenges and highest peaks and say, "Don't give up, you can do it. I'll be with you and help you."

When we take our eyes off our fears, our doubts, and our struggles to focus on someone else's needs, we somehow forget our own needs, at least for a little while. In believing the power of God's promises for others, our confidence in His promises for ourselves seems to grow as well. That is the power of encouraging words!

Where I Am From

As we live in the power of God's promises and move forward with confident hearts, it will be important for us to remember where we are from. How we let the past define us will be determined by the way we frame our memories. Will we frame them through our feelings of insecurity, or through the filter of God's assurances and promises?

When I became a mom for the first time, over sixteen years ago, I was overwhelmed. It wasn't just because of the amount of time and attention my baby needed, although that almost did me in. Instead, one of the hardest parts was the overwhelming love and responsibility I felt for my little guy. It literally made me cry to love someone that much.

As the years have passed, there have been so many things I wanted for my children. I wanted them to grow up knowing they are loved, valued, and created for God's purpose. I have prayed that they would find security as children of God and stability through a sense of belonging in our family.

I've been a very imperfect parent. But God gives me confidence to keep trying each day as I seek to love my kids like He loves me. The day after I freaked out about Joshua's dirty laundry fiasco, I apologized and asked for his forgiveness. He said he forgave me, and then he told me that he usually doesn't even remember things like that the next day.

Only God's perfect love could help my son keep no record of my wrongs. Several days later, I was reading through some of Joshua's writing assignments and found something that put it all into perspective. He gave me special permission to share it with you.

Where I Am From

I am from being outside.
I am from friends playing together.
I am from trampolines and wooden forts.
I am from imaginations combining together to create
    something marvelous.

I am from early Christmas mornings in front of the fire.
I am from Halloween in the back of a pickup.

I am from Easters at Grandma's.
I am from Uncle Bill's lake on the 4th of July.

I am from red beans and rice while watching *Moby
Dick* with a friend.
I am from eating huge piles of cheese fries from Out-
back with a former NFL player.
I am from crawfish and crab at Grandpa's house after
catching them.
I am from homemade chicken noodle soup that could
be mistaken to be from heaven.

I am from mistakes and successes.
I am from fun times and sad times.
I am from wonderful memories.
I am from a wonderful life.

And it's not even halfway done.[4]

This is a scrapbook of my child's life in his own words.
Not a picture of a perfect life, but snapshots of memories
that have given him security, stability, and perspective in the
midst of disappointments and struggles with his own doubts
and fears. Instead of focusing on those, he chose to define
where he is from with the faces of family and friends, special
traditions, and God's grace.

God used Joshua's words to remind me that I don't have
to be a perfect mom or a perfect woman. I just need to be
intentional and available to live and love well. Let's ask God
to remind us of this truth and redefine where we are from
as we allow the ink of His confidence and truth to write the
story of our lives.

I can't believe how far we've come together, or that this
part of our journey is coming to an end. My hope is that you
are and will keep on experiencing freedom from your doubts

and that your confidence is being richly rewarded, even now. Be sure to review chapter 12, where I have created a resource for us to use in the days ahead. I also hope you will take a minute to visit my interactive website at www.ReneeSwope .com and let me know what God has done through the words He gave me to share with you. I'd love to hear your story!

Do you mind if I pray for you? *I pray that the glorious Father, the God of our Lord Jesus Christ, would give you a spirit of wisdom and revelation as you come to know Christ better. Then you will have deeper insight. You will know the* **confidence** *that He calls you to have and the glorious wealth that God's people will inherit. You will also know the unlimited greatness of His power as it works with might and strength for us, the believers. In Jesus' name, Amen.* (Eph. 1:17–19)

Praying God's Promises

Lord, I want my life to be a love letter from Christ, written not with ink but with the Spirit of the living God, and not on tablets of stone but on the tablet of my heart. Holy Spirit, remind me that I have been crucified with Christ and I no longer live, but Christ lives in me. The life I live in my body, I live by faith in Him who loved me and gave Himself for me. You say that I'm precious and honored in Your sight. You call me Your beloved and tell me I can rest securely in You, for You shield me all day long.

Thank You for the exceedingly great and precious promises You have given me; through them I am a partaker in Your divine nature. I want to give away all that You have given me. Now to Him who is able to do immeasurably more than all I can ask or imagine, according to His power that is at work within me, to Him be glory in the church and in Christ

Jesus throughout all generations, for ever and ever! In Jesus' name, Amen.

See 2 Corinthians 3:3; Galatians 2:20; Isaiah 43:4; Deuteronomy 33:12; 2 Peter 1:4; Ephesians 3:20–21.

Reflection and Discussion Questions

1. Now that we have spent extended time getting to know God for who He truly is, let's see how our image of Him has changed. Close your eyes and think about God. Write down what you see and feelings you have.
2. Describe who you were when you started this book and compare her to the woman you are becoming as a result of learning and living in the power of God's promises.
3. Is she the woman you want to be? How will you continue your daily journey toward the heart of God and hold on to the security that is your birthright as a child of God?
4. "Like God did with Gideon, and like He does with us, we can come alongside others in some of life's hardest challenges and highest peaks and say, 'Don't give up, you can do it. I'll be with you and help you.'. . . In believing the power of God's promises for others, our confidence in His promises for ourselves seems to grow as well" (p. 216). Who will you pray for and encourage with your words, so that your confident heart in Christ becomes contagious? Who would God want you to reread this book with, so the message can sink deeper into your heart and be a catalyst for growing confidence in their heart?

I encourage you to pray God's promises at the end of each chapter again and again. Take time to say them out loud so that your heart, mind, and soul know without a doubt that you are committed to believing and living in their truth. Copy and post them where you will see them often, and pray them until they become a part of who you are!

12

Living in the Security of God's Promises

Everything that was written in the past was written to teach us, so that through the endurance taught in the Scriptures and the encouragement they provide we might have hope.

Romans 15:4

When I Say	God Says	Powerful Promises
I can't figure things out.	I will direct your steps.	Trust in the LORD with all your heart and lean not on your own understanding; in all your ways submit to him, and he will make your paths straight. (Prov. 3:5–6)
I'm too tired.	I will give you rest.	Come to me, all you who are weary and burdened, and I will give you rest. (Matt. 11:28)
I feel so weak.	I'll give you power.	My grace is sufficient for you, for my power is made perfect in weakness. (2 Cor. 12:9)

When I Say	God Says	Powerful Promises
My life is too hard.	Let Me help you.	I will be with him in trouble, I will deliver him and honor him. (Ps. 91:15)
Life is full of problems.	I am working for your good.	And we know that God causes everything to work together for the good of those who love God and are called according to his purpose for them. (Rom. 8:28 NLT)
This situation is impossible.	All things are possible with My help.	What is impossible with man is possible with God. (Luke 18:27)
I have nothing to give.	I will provide.	And God will generously provide all you need. Then you will always have everything you need and plenty left over to share with others. (2 Cor. 9:8 NLT)
I can't do it.	Rely on My strength and you can do all that I've called you to do.	I have strength for all things in Christ Who empowers me. (Phil. 4:13 AMP)
I feel so alone.	I will never leave you nor forsake you.	The LORD your God goes with you; he will never leave you nor forsake you. (Deut. 31:6)
I can't take this anymore.	I will supply all your needs.	And this same God who takes care of me will supply all your needs from his glorious riches, which have been given to us in Christ Jesus. (Phil. 4:19 NLT)
I'm too afraid.	I have not given you a spirit of fear.	For God has not given us a spirit of fear and timidity, but of power, love, and self-discipline. (2 Tim. 1:7 NLT)
My concerns are consuming me.	Cast all your cares on Me.	Give all your worries and cares to God, for he cares about you. (1 Pet. 5:7 NLT)
I feel overwhelmed.	I will give you peace.	I have told you these things, so that in Me you may have [perfect] peace and confidence. (John 16:33 AMP)

When I Say	God Says	Powerful Promises
I can't forgive myself.	I forgive you.	God is faithful and reliable. If we confess our sins, he forgives them and cleanses us from everything we've done wrong. (1 John 1:9 GW)
I don't have enough confidence.	I will be your confidence.	For the LORD will be your confidence and will keep your foot from being caught. (Prov. 3:26 NASB)
I'm not strong enough.	I am your strength.	God is the strength of my heart and my portion forever. (Ps. 73:26)
I don't know what to do.	I will give you wisdom.	If any of you lacks wisdom, you should ask God, who gives generously to all without finding fault, and it will be given to you. (James 1:5)
I feel so depressed.	Let My love and faithfulness guard your heart.	Because of the LORD's great love we are not consumed, for his compassions never fail. They are new every morning; great is [His] faithfulness. (Lam. 3:21–23)
I'll never change.	I am transforming you.	And we all, who with unveiled faces contemplate the Lord's glory, are being transformed into his image with ever-increasing glory, which comes from the Lord, who is the Spirit. (2 Cor. 3:18)
I feel condemned.	I will never condemn you.	So now there is no condemnation for those who belong to Christ Jesus. (Rom. 8:1 NLT)
I'll never be content.	You can learn to be content.	I have learned the secret of being content in any and every situation, whether well fed or hungry, whether living in plenty or in want. (Phil. 4:12)
I feel worthless.	You are precious and loved by Me.	You are precious and honored in my sight, and . . . I love you. (Isa. 43:4)
Everyone is against me.	I am for you!	If God is for us, who can be against us? (Rom. 8:31)

When I Say	God Says	Powerful Promises
I have no goals or purpose.	I have goals and purpose for your life.	My goal is that they may be encouraged in heart and united in love, so that they may have the full riches of complete understanding, in order that they may know the mystery of God, namely, Christ. (Col. 2:2)
I feel defeated.	You are a conqueror!	In all these things we are more than conquerors through him who loved us. (Rom. 8:37)
I can't stop sinning.	I offer you freedom.	Where the Spirit of the Lord is, there is freedom. (2 Cor. 3:17)
I just want to quit.	Be strong and do the work.	Be strong and courageous, and do the work. Don't be afraid or discouraged, for the LORD God, my God, is with you. He will not fail you or forsake you. (1 Chron. 28:20 NLT)
I'm nothing special.	You are a masterpiece.	For [you] are God's masterpiece. He has created us anew in Christ Jesus, so we can do the good things he planned for us long ago. (Eph. 2:10 NLT)
I'm not good enough.	You're royalty to Me.	You will be a crown of splendor in the LORD's hand, a royal diadem in the hand of your God. (Isa. 62:3)
I feel so ugly.	I think you're beautiful.	The king [is] enthralled by your beauty; honor him, for he is your lord. (Ps. 45:11)
I'm such a failure.	Your destiny is victory!	But I thank God, who always leads us in victory because of Christ. (2 Cor. 2:14 GW)

Notes

Chapter 2 Because God's Love Is Perfect, I Don't Have to Be

1. Eldredge, John and Brent Curtis, *The Sacred Romance* (Nashville: Thomas Nelson, 1997), 83.

Chapter 3 Finding Love That Won't Fail Even When I Do

1. http://dictionary.reference.com/browse/worship.

Chapter 4 God Promises Hope for My Future Despite the Pain of My Past

1. Eldredge and Curtis, *Sacred Romance*, 158.
2. Scripture from Isaiah 61 is taken from the 1984 edition of the New International Version®. NIV®. Copyright © 1973, 1978, 1984 by Biblica, Inc.™ Used by permission of Zondervan. All rights reserved worldwide. www.zondervan.com.

Chapter 6 When Doubt Whispers "I'm Not Good Enough"

1. Dr. Neil T. Anderson, *Victory Over the Darkness* (Ventura, CA: Regal Books, 1990), 48.
2. http://newlife919blog.blogs.com/new_life_919_blog/2009/06/my-bully.html.
3. "God Is In Control," © 1993 by Twila Paris. All Rights Reserved. From *He Is Exalted: Live Worship* CD.

Chapter 7 When Doubt Whispers "I'm Such a Failure"

1. Dr. Neil T. Anderson, "Daily In Christ," posted August 10, 2010, http://www.crosswalk.com/devotionals/dailyinchrist/544718/.

2. Zig Ziglar, *Raising Positive Kids in a Negative World* (New York: Ballantine, 1989), 51.

3. "Mining for Gold in the Heart of Your Child Character Chart," http:// shopp31.com/miningforgoldintheheartofyourchildcdandcharacterchart.aspx.

Chapter 8 When Doubt Whispers "I Don't Have Anything Special to Offer"

1. Florence Littauer, *Personality Plus* (Grand Rapids: Revell, 1992).

2. Bruce Bugbee, *What You Do Best in the Body of Christ* (Grand Rapids: Zondervan, 1995), 31.

3. For more information on Beth Moore studies, visit Living Proof Ministries at www.lproof.com.

4. Lysa TerKeurst, *Living Life on Purpose* (Chicago: Moody, 2000), 51.

Chapter 9 When Doubt Whispers "I Can't Stop Worrying"

1. Sarah Young, *Jesus Calling: Enjoying Peace in His Presence* (Nashville: Thomas Nelson, 2004), 17.

2. Max Lucado, *Come Thirsty* (Nashville: W Publishing Group, 2004), 101.

3. http://gobible.com.

Chapter 10 When Doubt Whispers "I Can't Follow God Consistently"

1. Lysa TerKeurst, *Becoming More Than a Good Bible Study Girl* (Grand Rapids: Zondervan, 2009), 145. Lysa also offers a free downloadable resource on her website at www.LysaTerKeurst.com entitled, "When God Hurts My Feelings," which offers additional insights to help you process your "why" questions with God.

Chapter 11 The Woman I Want to Be

1. Beth Moore, *So Long Insecurity* (Carol Stream, IL: Tyndale, 2010), 311.

2. Melissa Taylor, "Is God Enough?" *Encouragement for Today*, http://proverbs 31devotions.blogspot.com/2010/07/is-god-enough.html. Posted July 2, 2010.

3. Melissa Taylor, "13 Years Ago Today," http://melissataylor.org/2010/07/02/13 -years-ago-today. Posted July 2, 2010.

4. "Where I Am From," © 2009, Joshua Swope.

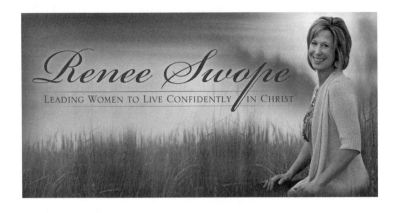

Renee Swope is a national women's conference speaker and former co-host of Proverbs 31 Ministries' international radio program. Like having coffee with a friend and mentor, Renee's authentic style and soul-stirring messages draw women closer to the heart of God and each other.

Through her written and spoken words, Renee shares from a heart that has been transformed by the power of God's love and grace. Weaving in personal stories and spiritual life lessons, Renee's topics speak to the challenges women face, the heartaches and joys they share. Sprinkled with humor and saturated with Truth, Renee's messages are filled with Biblical insights that are powerful and life-applications that are practical as she seeks to help women:

- Identify paralyzing self-doubts and replace them with transforming truths
- Discern God's voice and recognize His direction in their daily decisions
- Let go of past pain and take hold of their promised identity and security in Christ

- Turn worry into worship by shifting their focus from "what if" towards "what is"
- Transform fear-filled thinking into faith-filled believing by actively trusting God's promises in their everyday lives and relationships

Renee lives with her family in North Carolina with her husband and three children.

Invite Renee to speak at your next women's event!
Your audience will be challenged as women and encouraged as children of God!

www.ReneeSwope.com
For more information or to personally connect with Renee, visit her interactive website.

Dig Deep into Scripture
and Transform the Way You Parent

Continue your journey
with Renee Swope toward
a more confident heart with
a 60-day devotional

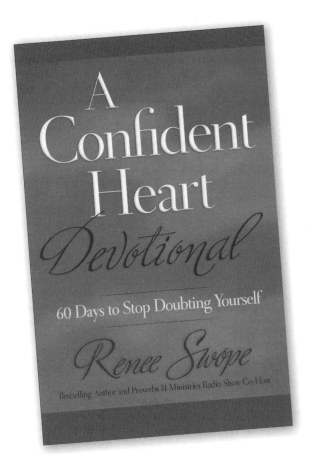

JOIN RENEE

for personal encouragement to help you live with a confident heart!

Visit ReneeSwope.com

to download free resources and watch videos to enhance your personal study, share with your small group, or contribute to your book club. You can also see Renee's speaking schedule or join the next *A Confident Heart* online study.

f A Confident Heart by Renee Swope
f Renee Swope 🐦 ReneeSwope 📷 ReneeSwope